# INSIDE
# BOXING

# INSIDE
# BOXING

## Robert Seltzer

## MetroBooks

# MetroBooks

An Imprint of Friedman/Fairfax Publishers

©2000 by Michael Friedman Publishing Group, Inc.

Library of Congress Cataloging-in-Publication Data

Seltzer, Robert.
    Inside boxing / Robert Seltzer.
        p. cm.
    Includes index.
    ISBN  1-56799-821-6
    1. Boxing—United States—History—20th century. 2. Boxers (Sports)—United
States—Biography. I. Title.

GV1125 .S45 2000
796.83--dc21

                                                                        99-059128

Editor: Benjamin Mott
Art Director: Jeff Batzli
Designer: Charles Donahue
Photography Editor: Valerie Kennedy
Production Managers: Camille Lee and Maria Gonzalez

Color separations by Leefung Asco Repro Ltd. Co.
Printed in China by Leefung Asco Printers Ltd.

1 3 5 7 9 10 8 6 4 2

For bulk purchases and special sales, please contact:
Friedman/Fairfax Publishers
Attention: Sales Department
15 West 26th Street
New York, NY 10010
212/685-6610  FAX 212/685-1307

Visit our website:
www.metrobooks.com

## *Dedication*

To the three most wonderful people in my little corner of the world.

## *Acknowledgments*

Boxing is the most brutal sport in the world, a sport that makes football and hockey look like a Thursday afternoon bridge game. But exploring its history has been a rich, enlightening endeavor, one in which I was assisted by friends and colleagues throughout the country.

I owe a huge debt to Gary Miles, a fine writer and editor at the *Philadelphia Inquirer*. Without his help and recommendation, this book would not have been possible. I also would like to thank all my editors at Barnes & Noble Publishing, especially Nathaniel Marunas, who provided invaluable help as we reached the end of the project.

I began researching this book long before I knew I would write it. And for that, I want to thank my fellow sportswriters, men who shared their wisdom with me in bars and arenas throughout the country, sometimes thoughtfully, sometimes sardonically, but always with a passion and insight that stamped them as experts. They include men like Ed Schuyler, Jr., Pat Putnam, Royce Feour, Joe Maxse, Tom Archdeacon, Tom Loverro, Tim Kawakami, Chris Thorne, Wallace Matthews, Bill Stickney, Ron Borges, Bert Sugar, Michael Katz, and many more.

For every editor who has ever struggled with my prose on deadline, especially Gary Howard, now the sports editor of the *Milwaukee Journal Sentinel*, I would like to extend my hand…and sympathy.

I thank Bill Knight and Robert Holguin, who provided both encouragement and advice throughout this project. I also would like to thank the management of the *El Paso Times*, especially executive editor Dionicio "Don" Flores, who has always encouraged boxing coverage in the sports section of his paper. I am indebted, also, to Nora Salazar and Judy Soles McMillie, both of whom are as efficient as they are patient. And a special thank you to Lulu Ballesteros, whose heart is as broad as her smile.

Finally, I would like to thank three of the finest writers I have known…my Dad, who encouraged my love of books and boxing; my daughter, Katy, who once wrote her own (condensed) version of *Animal Farm* for a grade school English assignment; and my son, Christopher, who once consoled me over an editorial I had written, saying, "Don't worry, Dad. I know there's not much room for poetry in the newspaper business."

—El Paso, Texas, June 2000

PAGE 2: Oscar De La Hoya and Felix Trinidad (both of whom were undefeated welterweight champions at the time thanks to today's infinitely subdivided championship belts) squared off in one of the modern era's most highly anticipated fights on September 18, 1999. ABOVE: Two of the great lightweights of their day shake hands before a fight: powerful left-hander Lew Tendler (left) and ring legend Benny Leonard. These men fought two epic bouts, one in 1922 and the next almost a year later to the day, in 1923. The first fight was ruled a no-decision after 12 rounds, and the second was won by Leonard, by decision, after 15. Born Benjamin Leiner in 1896, Leonard was one of the greatest lightweights ever to step into the ring. He was a near-perfect balance of power, speed, agility, and strategy; moreover, he was a successful Jewish fighter at a time when Jews were discouraged from participating in professional boxing. Leonard defended the lightweight crown for an amazing stretch of 7 years, 7 months. PAGES 6–7: Rocky Marciano folds Jersey Joe Wolcott over with a murderous left to the midsection during the 4th round of their famous title bout on September 23, 1952.

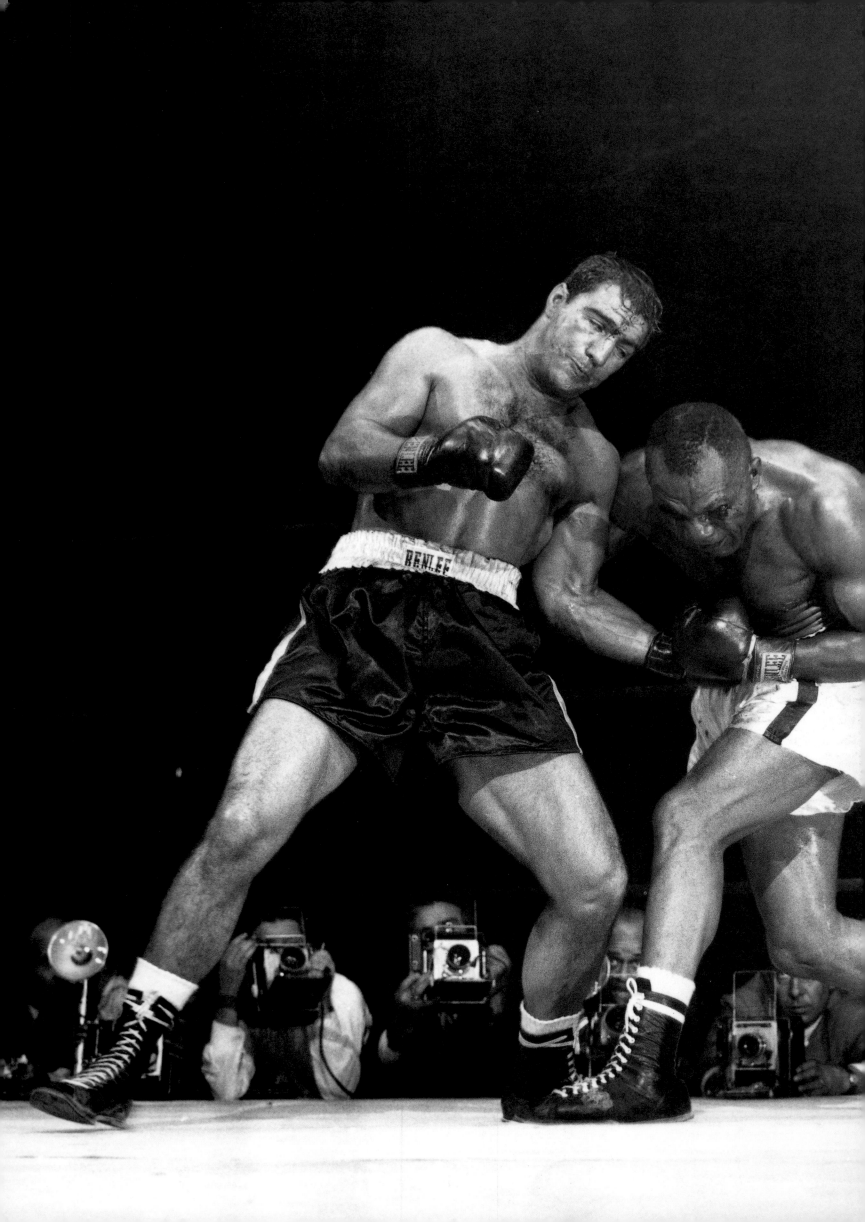

# CONTENTS

# INTRODUCTION

If boxing ever became a kind of fencing with fists, a mere trial of skills, reflexes and agility, and not the test of courage, will and resilience that it is now, then it would lose its appeal for many who are neither sadists nor seekers after the trappings of virility.

—Hugh McIlvanney

Hell is not roped off. The ring is. And that may be the only difference between the two venues. Boxing is a ballistic ballet, a sport that can be lovely one minute, ugly the next. The beauty? Well, it is embodied in wondrous athletes such as Sugar Ray Robinson and Muhammad Ali, both of whom turned the ring into a ballroom, their movements so precise they appeared to be choreographed. But the beauty is everywhere, even in less graceful boxers such as Julio Cesar Chavez. He was not a dancer, but he was a marvel in his prime, his skills as subtle as they were incandescent—a dip of the shoulder here, a twitch of the head there. Poetry in motion? Well, yes, but it was more than that. It was poetry in commotion, because boxing is the most devious sport of all. Great boxers are great con men. They lead their opponents into thinking that they will do one thing, only to turn around and do another. They are pickpockets, not muggers.

Who could forget, for example, Ali performing his rope-a-dope routine against George Foreman in Zaire, Africa, during the legendary "Rumble in the Jungle" on October 30, 1974? Ali leaned against the ropes, a move that invited Foreman to pound his tender ribs. Ah, but there was one thing Foreman did not count on: those ribs, those inviting ribs, were not as vulnerable as his own psyche. Foreman, who would prove to be a wiser man during his comeback years, fell into a trap that night. Yes, Ali looked like a human percussion instrument, daring to get pounded by a bigger, stronger, younger man. But it was Foreman, not Ali, who got thumped. The heavyweight champion, sapped from punching an opponent who refused to wilt, grew fatigued in the middle rounds, his arms so heavy they seemed welded to his sides. And then, in the 8th round, Ali struck, knocking out the champion with a thunderbolt of a right hand. Foreman landed on his back and, struggling to his feet, looked up at the African sky, almost as if he thought the punch had emerged from the heavens. Perhaps it had. The pickpocket had overwhelmed the mugger; the beauty had conquered the brute. "Muhammad outsmarted me," Foreman would say years later. "That's all there is to it."

But if boxing can be as lovely as ballet, it can also be as brutal as a brawl in a back alley. For every Ali, Robinson, and Chavez, there is a pug out there, somewhere, intent on disgracing the sport that the great champions have elevated to

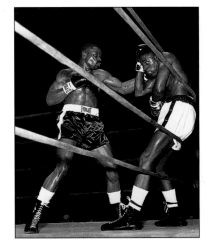

OPPOSITE: Sugar Ray Robinson, his trunks stained with blood, is declared the winner in his brutal battle for the middleweight crown against Jake La Motta on February 14, 1951. The first and only person to have beaten Robinson up until then? La Motta, who had pulled the feat off way back on February 5, 1943.
ABOVE: Rubin "Hurricane" Carter drives a cowering George Benton into the ropes during their 10-round bout on May 25, 1963, in New York City. Although Benton was the higher ranked middleweight going into the fight, Carter won the split decision over the Philadelphia native. Both men would go on to become quite famous, Carter as the long-suffering victim of a racist miscarriage of the U.S. judicial system (he was falsely convicted of a triple homicide and sent to prison for nineteen years) and Benton as one of the great trainers of his day.

LEFT: Muhammad Ali and Joe Frazier, two of the greatest heavyweight fighters in history, beam for the cameras. Though their bouts are the stuff that boxing legends are made of, and though they maintained a heated feud out of the ring (mainly due to the rigors of self-promotion), it is tempting to think that the two men would have been good friends in another life.

art. Is Mike Tyson, the former heavyweight champion of the world, the greatest pug in boxing history? Perhaps that is too harsh. Yes, he has been guilty of repulsive and illegal behavior, but he has paid for that behavior. Tyson is a lonely, confused, miserable man, his insecurities so profound that he should have a psychiatrist in his corner. But boxing is an unforgiving sport, and nobody knows that better than Tyson, the terror of the heavyweight division from 1986 to 1990. Tyson lost his title, and then he lost his freedom, receiving a three-year prison sentence for raping a teenage beauty contestant on July 19, 1991. When he

OPPOSITE: Behold a scene from one of the most fabled fights of modern boxing history, when a resurgent Muhammad Ali rose from the ashes of his banishment from professional boxing and scorched the heavily favored George Foreman to reclaim the heavyweight championship in 1974. In this shot from the 5th round of the so-called "Rumble in the Jungle," Foreman slips a left through Ali's defenses and catches the challenger on the jaw. ABOVE: On September 7, 1996, Mike Tyson mauls Bruce Seldon in the 1st round; a few seconds later, Tyson knocked Seldon out to capture the heavyweight title. The victory recalled Tyson's swift rise through the heavyweight ranks as an up-and-comer; he was so good for a stretch in the mid-1980s that most observers thought he was on the way to becoming one of the best ever.

came back in 1995, he was not the "Iron Mike" who had knocked out 35 opponents and left a trail of prone bodies in his wake.

Evander Holyfield stripped Tyson of his heavyweight title on November 9, 1996, in Las Vegas, and ripped off the cloak of invincibility "Iron Mike" had worn throughout much of his comeback. It was one of the biggest upsets in boxing history, but one man refused to be shocked, and he was the only man who counted—Holyfield. Who could blame him? Holyfield, after all, was no Bruce Seldon, the self-proclaimed "Atlantic City Express." Seldon met Tyson on September 7, 1996, in Las Vegas, but Seldon fought as if he wanted to win an Oscar, not a boxing match. Tyson landed a right to the jaw early in the 1st round, and Seldon performed a rumba, his legs moving independently of his torso. Tyson fired again and again, and the rumba intensified, becoming a rhythmic dance to the beat of the pounding Seldon felt in his head.

# THE SPORT

**1**

"Cowardice disgusts you, no matter where it happens, no matter what form it takes. Bravery exalts a man. It can be pointless and done for dirty reasons, but the act itself never has demeaned the human race, although it is possible the motives may sicken you."
—Jimmy Cannon, *Nobody Asked Me, But...*

The origins of the sport of boxing are as dark and murky as a cave, which was probably the venue for the first match in boxing history. Think of it, two cave men performing in front of their tribes, their clans—the ancestors of Roberto Duran and Sugar Ray Leonard. If that sounds far-fetched, remember that boxing is the most visceral, brutal and, thus, primitive sport in the world. Every day, in bars and back alleys from Altoona, Pennsylvania, to Waco, Texas, to Lodi, California, men get arrested for doing what it is perfectly legal to do in the ring—beat the hell out of each other. And they have been doing it for centuries, thus continuing a tradition that started when the first pugilists made fists in a cave.

But is that really a sport? Is that really an art, as the great writer A.J. Liebling claimed? Does a guy in a white shirt and a black bow tie, also known as a referee, truly bring civility to an activity that seems so uncivilized? The answer is a resounding "yes." Liebling was right. Boxing is an art. Why? Because of men like Muhammad Ali and Sugar Ray Robinson. If Baryshnikov had been able to hook off the jab—and brag about it afterwards—he, not Ali, would have been "The Greatest." But it was Ali, a ballet artist with attitude, who lifted his sport to the ozone. "Me. We!" Ali once recited in the shortest poem he ever wrote—an ode to his favorite subject, himself.

But there were no Alis, no Robinsons, when the sport originated in those dark, gloomy caves. It was a grim, brutal activity, unrefined by art or humor or round-card girls. There were no million-dollar paychecks, no ring announcers, no promoters whose hair defied gravity. No, there were just two guys fighting for honor or food or territory. It was prehistoric mayhem.

Ancient stone carvings indicate that the Sumerians, who lived in what is now Iraq, boxed at least five thousand years ago. They were the forerunners of Ali and Robinson, and they spread the activity to other parts of the ancient world, including Greece, where the sport became a brutal, ugly spectacle. Two men would sit on flat stones, face to face, mano a mano, with their fists wrapped in strips of leather. There was a signal, the ancient equivalent of the opening bell, and the two men would batter each other until one of them fell to the ground, unconscious,

**OPPOSITE:** John Sholto Douglas, the Marquess of Queensberry, changed boxing forever by bringing order to the chaos that had reigned in the boxing matches of his day. He lived in England from 1844 to 1900, but his rules became the foundation for the sport as the entire world came to know it.
**ABOVE:** Light heavyweight Harry Greb, "the Pittsburgh Windmill," was one of the most ferocious fighters of his day, a boxer who rained physical abuse on his opponents in such frightening fashion that one writer described his style as "the Manly Art of Modified Murder." He was the only boxer to beat Gene Tunney, and he beat him severely, winning the light heavyweight crown in the process. Amazingly, Greb (born Edward Henry Berg) fought the last five years of his career blind in one eye, a fact he concealed. Tragically, Greb died at the age of 32 on the operating table.

ABOVE: The ancient Greeks were avid practitioners of boxing, as this vase, which dates from the 6th century B.C., clearly illustrates. Note the leather wrapping around the contestants' fists; the Romans would later "improve" on this by weighting the leather (the *cesti*) with lead and in some cases even adding spikes.

as flat as a cardboard cut-out. But that was not always the end of it. The winner would sometimes continue to pound his victim until he died.

In ancient Rome, a brutal sport became even more brutal. The boxers wore *cesti*, leather straps plated with metal, on their hands and forearms. It was an ugly, diabolical game. The contestants did not need swords, spears, or tridents, because their own limbs were the weapons; the slightest movement, the slightest forearm shiver, could blind or kill an opponent. But the brutality would not last; developed as a spectator sport, it eventually outraged the spectators, including the officers who developed it. Approximately 100 years before the birth of Christ, the Romans banned the sport.

The sport re-emerged in the early 1700s, when James Figg, one of the most famous athletes in England, introduced modern boxing to the world. He opened a boxing school in London, a latter-day gladiator camp, teaching his students the style that would become known as bare-knuckle fighting. But how did he arrive at a style that had eluded centuries of pugilists before him? Figg was a wrestler, but in one of those acts of serendipity that bridge the old world to the new, he grew tired of half-nelson this and full-nelson that, and he threw a punch. Yes, a punch. It may have been a jab or a hook or a cross—or, perhaps, a silly, awkward hybrid of all three. We are not sure. What is certain is that Figg started it all, helping to launch the procession of boxers that leads to contemporary champions such

as welterweight dynamo Felix Trinidad. It was a modest beginning, but a beginning nonetheless.

In 1743, Jack Broughton yanked the sport one step—one bob and weave—closer to the twentieth century. He introduced rules to a sport that gloried in its lack of rules, and these codes became standards for all boxing matches. They were known as the London Prize Ring Rules, and they helped make the sport more civilized, although they may not seem civilized to contemporary boxing fans. One rule, for example, required that boxers continue to fight, without rest periods, until one man could no longer go on. Brutal? Undoubtedly. But the rules were intended to attract the nobility to this savage sport. Broughton also conducted boxing classes at the Haymarket Academy in London, advertising them as instructions in the mystery of boxing, the wholly British art for gentlemen.

And then it happened. In 1872, John Sholto Douglas—a British sportsman also known as the Marquess of Queensberry—sponsored a new boxing code. It was revolutionary, and the Marquess of Queensberry, building on the modest cornerstone of his compatriot James Figg, launched the modern era in the sport. John Sholto Douglas was to boxing what Elvis Presley was to rock 'n' roll—a dynamic figure who altered, forever, his chosen profession, his chosen world. The rules were so brilliantly simple that they have been taken for granted by every succeeding generation of boxers and fans. They required boxers to wear gloves, a requirement which would cut down on the brutal injuries that made the contestants look like walking hematomas. They called for three-minute rounds, rather than the one long continuous flurry of action under the old rules, with a one-minute rest period between rounds. The rules also stated that a man down on one knee could not be struck, and that a fallen man must be given 10 seconds to get back on his feet.

Pierce Egan, the great historian of what he called "boxiana," coined the term "the sweet science" in 1824. It was a lovely term, lending credibility to a sport filled with loutish brutes. But was it accurate? Egan detected a beauty, an artistry, in the sport, but he saw science and strategy where most fans saw chaos and mayhem. And the reason was simple—the sport was decades away from the revolution that the Marquess of Queensberry would engineer. And, even after the Marquess of Queensberry rules, the sport was slow to enact the code; some fights were waged under the rules, others were not, and that was true for both England and the United States. There was no rhyme or reason, no governing body, to legitimize the sport, to make sense of it. It was as haphazard, as unrefined, as a street fight.

"Sweet science" indeed. The sport was neither sweet nor scientific. Professional bouts were glorified cockfights, with the boxing matches staged on carnival or circus grounds, the "ring" provided by fans who held hands to form a wall of humanity. There were no rest periods, and fights lasted until one of the pugs, battered and exhausted, could no longer continue. Some fighters were so brutish that they frowned on throwing punches. Why be so elegant, so dainty, when tactics such as gouging, biting, and kicking were more effective?

It was out of this brutal environment that the great John L. Sullivan emerged. He was a neighborhood bully, but his neighborhood was the world—an area as vast as his ego. "I can lick any sumbitch in the house," he liked to say, and he was right. He stood 5-feet-11 (180cm) and weighed 180 pounds (82kg), and every ounce seemed to be concentrated in his right hand, which could unleash a lightning bolt of a punch. But the great John L. was not just a sporting figure; he was a social figure, famous for his exploits both inside and outside the ring. And what were those exploits? He was a drunk, a glutton, a bully, and a wife beater—and, yes, the country loved him, making him the first sports superstar of the American landscape, a Babe Ruth in short pants. But why? Why elevate a man so vile and despicable, a man who scorned all the qualities the country seemed to treasure—trust, loyalty, generosity, good will?

An Irish-American from a working class background in Roxbury, Massachusetts, he embodied the raw spirit of the country, a country that seemed without limits as it pushed westward in the late 1800s. The nation was exploding during the Industrial Revolution; according to the U.S. Census of 1880, New York became the first city to top one million. One million. If that was not exhilarating, if that did not fill you with pride, then, dammit, you were not an American. This was the United States of America, big and tough and sprawling, and nobody symbolized that toughness more than the great John L. himself. A scoundrel and a wastrel, he fought for liquor as readily as for cash,

Dapper in a dark suit, John L. Sullivan—"The Boston Strongboy," "The Hercules of the Ring," "The Prizefighting Caesar," "His Fistic Highness"—cuts a remarkably civilized figure for a man who became a legend by striding across the American cultural landscape smashing his bare fists into the faces of his opponents.

There was only one problem: the first blow landed, but the subsequent punches missed—finding air, not flesh. But Seldon did not care; he continued to dance, continued to feign a mild concussion, because he wanted the referee to stop the match. The referee finally obliged. The fight—no, the performance—lasted 109 seconds.

No, Holyfield was no Bruce Seldon. He performed no rumbas against Tyson. The fight was a dance, all right, but it was the ballistic ballet that all boxing fans crave. Holyfield pounded Tyson for 11 rounds, and the last blow was the cruelest of all—a right hand that sent Tyson into the ropes, battered and bloodied, his arms dangling like the sleeves of an empty jacket. The referee stopped the bout 37 seconds into the 11th round. Afterward, Tyson was uncharacteristically gracious. "He's a good fighter," Tyson said, still dazed, at the postfight press conference. "I'd like to fight him again."

The grace and dignity did not last long. Tyson and Holyfield met again on June 28, 1997, in Las Vegas—one of the wildest farces in boxing history. Tyson, unable to subdue Holyfield with his fists, resorted to his teeth. He bit the champion on both ears, took a chunk out of the right one, then spit it out as if it were a piece of gristle. The referee stopped the bout at the end of the 3rd round, when both fouls occurred. "I wanted to kill him," Tyson would say later. Tyson turned Holyfield into steak tartare, and the world recoiled in horror. The Nevada Athletic Commission responded swiftly and decisively, fining the fighter $3 million and revoking his license for one year. "I just snapped," Tyson said.

The great sportswriter Jimmy Cannon called boxing "the red-light district" of sports, and Tyson seemed to reinforce what critics had long suspected—that boxing is a sewer minus the manhole cover. But is it really? If Tyson lowered the sport, Holyfield elevated it. The champion forgave Tyson, confirming that Holyfield is a man of uncommon class and dignity, in clear contrast to his opponent. This act was the only saving grace to the sad, shabby episode of the biting incident—and a clear victory for the sport of boxing.

LEFT: Evander Holyfield, standing up to the man he branded a "bully," lands a right uppercut en route to his 11th-round knockout of Mike Tyson on November 9, 1996. Over the course of the rivalry between these two fighters, the behaviour of the devoutly religious and soft-spoken Holyfield proved to be the perfect antidote to Tyson's disreputable behavior and shrill pronouncements.

# The Confusing World of Champions

In an age when fighters collect world titles as if they were postage stamps, the great boxers of yesterday—Jack Dempsey, Joe Louis, Sugar Ray Robinson—would be aghast.

Every last one of them would cringe at what is happening to their sport because they fought in an era in which there were eight weight classes, each division represented by one—count them, one—world champion.

Today, it has come to this: there are seventeen weight classes, and everybody but your cousin Fred is a champion of something or other.

Does that sound like an exaggeration?

Well, consider the number of organizations that sponsor world champions: there is the IBF, the WBA, the WBC, the WBO, the IBO, the IBC, the WBF, the WBU, the...

Is there an Elks Lodge in your area?

An American Legion Post?

A post office?

A bar?

They probably sponsor world champions, too.

And if you multiply the weight classes by the number of sanctioning bodies, that means there are almost as many world champions as there are fans to pay for their fights.

"It's ridiculous," says Eddie Futch, the former trainer, now 88. "The boxing organizations are worthless. I don't know how the public buys all of their shenanigans."

It has become so absurd that Eric Esch, also known as "Butterbean," is a champion—never mind that this "champ" boasts all the mobility of a heavy bag. He weighs more than 300 pounds, qualifying him as a human land mass, but he is not the heavyweight champion. No, he is the heavyweight champion of the four-rounder. Yes, he is an undercard fighter who reigns as a "world titlist," and his championship belt is as impressive as the belly that he cinches it around—you could tow a truck with that belt. Butterbean is sanctioned by the International Boxing Association, a fledgling group that does not boast many quality fighters. Butterbean makes about $50,000 per fight, about as much as strawweight champion Ricardo Lopez, one of

the greatest fighters in the world, earns—a travesty to both Lopez and the sport he loves. But that is boxing for you.

"We know Butterbean's not a serious contender," said Dean Chance, a former major league pitcher who won the Cy Young award in 1964 and now runs the IBA. "But he's a great guy, and he's entertaining, and that's what it's all about." Is there anything wrong with that? Certainly not. Boxing has always boasted its share of entertainers: witness Chuck Wepner, the "Bayonne Bleeder," and Randall "Tex" Cobb, who took a brutal beating from then world heavyweight champion Larry Holmes on November 26, 1982, in Houston. Holmes, hugging the beaten fighter after the bout, offered him a rematch. "Sure," Cobb replied, "but next time we fight in a phone booth."

The entertainment is here to stay, and that is good. But the days when there were only eight weight classes are gone, and that is too bad. Not that boxing is devoid of quality champions, not at all. The sport still boasts fighters who could reign in almost any era—Evander Holyfield, Roy Jones, Felix Trinidad, Oscar De La Hoya.

So it is wrong to be bitter and crusty, looking at the old days as if they were the only days. It is just that, well, the world of champions was a lot less complicated when there were only eight weight classes. And only one champion in each class.

Eric Esch, the overweight boxer better known as Butterbean, blocks a punch with his head during a fight against Troy Roberts on September 18, 1998.

John L. Sullivan

and the fans loved him for it. And why not? The citizens were conquering the country, and Sullivan was conquering every man in the house—it was a strange but ideal marriage.

Born decades too early to exploit scientific training regimens, Sullivan knew nothing about aerobics or weight training, not to mention diet and nutrition. Sullivan ingested calories at a pace that would add 30 or 40 pounds to his frame between fights, but he knew nothing about nutrition or metabolism. And what if he had been born in a later generation? What if he had been able to take advantage of modern training methods? Sullivan would have spit on modern training methods, just as he spit on opponents. He would sooner train with a drinking buddy than with a fitness guru. Tough guys drink, right? And Sullivan was a tough guy. He trained by walking mile after mile through the working class neighborhoods of Boston, stopping at every saloon along the way. If his right hand delivered a thunderous punch, and it did, it was from his version of weight lifting—the constant repetitions with a mug of beer, up and down, from the bar to his throat, over and over again. The great John L. could drink as passionately as he could fight. By modern standards, Sullivan was soft and fleshy, his belly bulging over pants so tight that they looked like a second layer of skin. But, belly or no belly, he impressed the sporting public. Fans were blinded by his aura. They looked at a fat guy, but they saw a statue, a man with the hard physique of a coal miner. They saw a legend.

"Look at the Statue," wrote John Boyle O'Reilly. "That is Sullivan, life, body and spirit. See the tremendous chest, filled with capacious lungs and a mighty heart, capable of pumping blood everywhere at once. See the ponderous fist and the massive wrist; and the legs and feet—ah! there you see the limbs of a perfect boxer—light as a dancer, firm as a tower. And then, look up to the buttressed, Samson neck, springing beautifully from the great shoulders; look at the head—large, round as a Greek's, broad-browed, wide-

chinned, with a deep dimple, showing the good nature, and a mouth and lips that ought to be cut in granite, so full are they of doomful power and purpose."

Sullivan, already proclaiming himself the heavyweight champion of the world, yearned to prove it—not in the saloons, where he made his boasts, but in the ring, where his fists could make good on those boasts. He challenged Paddy Ryan, the true heavyweight champion of the world, deriding him from the pages of every sports section on the East Coast. Ryan finally relented. He met Sullivan in an outdoor arena on February 7, 1882, in New Orleans, Louisiana, where the *New Orleans Picayune* regretted that there was "no legal remedy to avert the disgusting spectacle," since an anti-boxing bill had been stalled in the legislature.

It may have been a "disgusting spectacle," but at least it was a short one. The fans had no sooner settled into their seats than Ryan was being deposited on his. The great John L. landed a right to the jaw, sending Ryan to the floor a mere 30 seconds after the fight started. Ryan struggled to his feet, but he would go down eight more times. The final knockdown came less than 11 minutes after the fight started, with Ryan sprawled on his back, as flat as an ink blot. His handlers threw in the sponge, the flag of surrender that would be replaced by the towel, and the sport crowned a new heavyweight champion of the world, bare-knuckle style—Sullivan could not only lick any sumbitch in the house, he could lick any sumbitch in the world. He was 23 years old.

OPPOSITE: Heavyweight champion John L. Sullivan, seen in this 1885 photograph striking a pugilistic pose in front of a woodsy backdrop, was a hero thanks to his exploits in and out of the ring. He was the last and greatest of the bare-knuckle champions. RIGHT: "Gentleman" Jim Corbett was the first boxing champion of the new breed: he trained heavily, used strategy to win fights, and fought wearing gloves. This photograph was taken in 1894, two years after his historic defeat of John L. Sullivan in what was the first official heavyweight bout to be fought under the Marquess of Queensberry rules.

RIGHT: This rare photograph (perhaps the only existing one ever taken of such a fight) shows the last official bare-knuckle bout in history, waged between John L. Sullivan and Jake Kilrain in a ring in rural Richburg, Mississippi, on July 8, 1889. Sullivan finally pounded Kilrain badly enough in the 75th round of the heavyweight title fight that Kilrain's trainers threw in the sponge before the next round could begin.

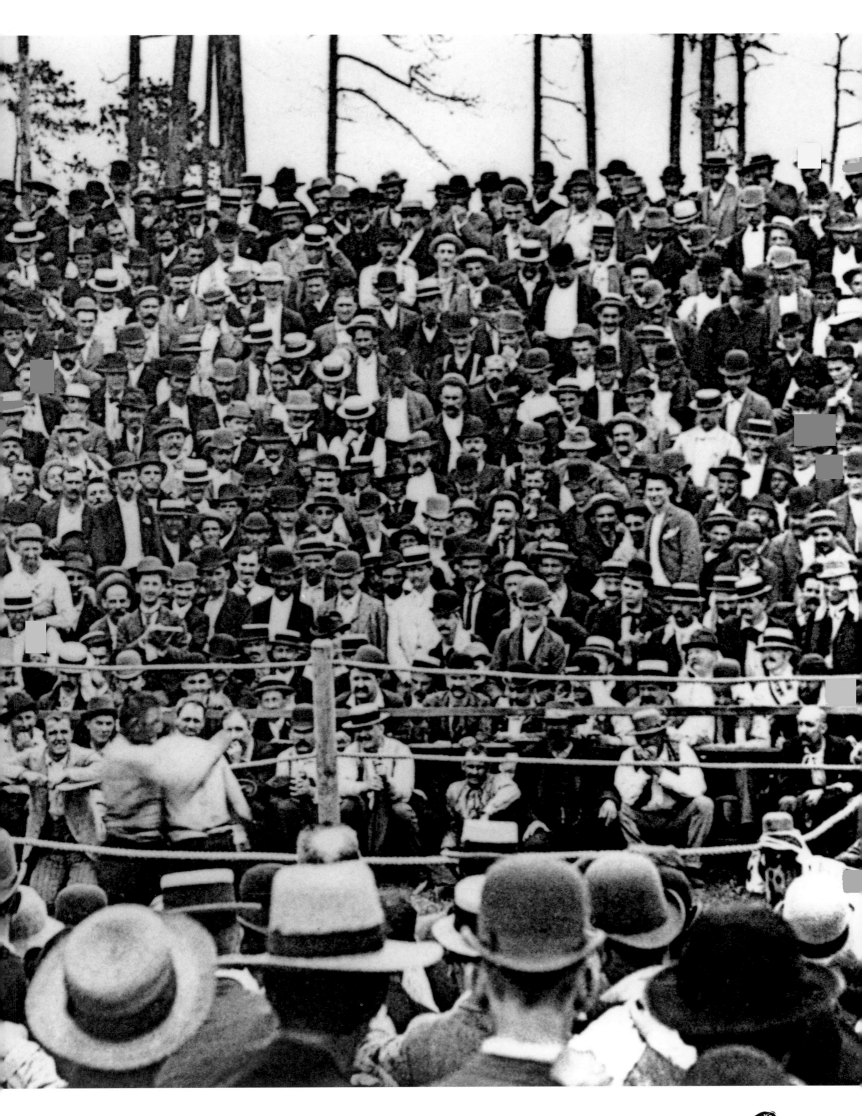

ABOVE: Known as "The Old Master," Joe Gans (right) was one of the slickest boxers of the early twentieth century. Here, Gans poses for the camera with challenger Mike "Twin" Sullivan in 1906. Born Joseph Gaines in 1874, Gans got his early pugilistic education in Baltimore, where he was prize fighting while just a teenager. At the age of 17, Gans won a rematch against lightweight champion Frank Erne with a knockout in the 1st round. By doing so, Gans became only the second fighter in modern history to win a championship in the 1st round and the first African-American ever to win the lightweight crown. Gans was one of the most scientific boxers of his day: he would carefully study his opponents to discover their weaknesses and then mercilessly put his observations to use in the ring. Sadly, this boxing pioneer died of tuberculosis at the tender age of 36. LEFT: Heavyweight Jack Johnson was one of boxing's trailblazers, as much for his talent as for his defiance of the status quo. At a time when integrated fights were frowned upon and popular opinion held that no black man could ever win the heavyweight championship, Johnson arranged to battle Tommy Burns for the crown. The landmark fight took place on December 26, 1908, in Sydney, Australia, and proved to be a mainly one-sided affair. Johnson brutalized Burns for almost 14 rounds before the local police brought the slaughter to a stop. Here, Johnson sizes up Burns during their famous bout.

On July 8, 1889, about seven years after he won the bare-knuckle title, Sullivan waged the last bare-knuckle fight in history. He met Jake Kilrain under a broiling sun near Biloxi, Mississippi, a spot now marked by a historical sign off the Gulf Coast, on Interstate Highway 12. "This is it," Bert Sugar, the boxing historian known for his prose and his cigar, would say 100 years later, standing only a foot from the sign. "This is it."

If Sugar regarded the site as a shrine, it is no wonder. The Sullivan-Kilrain match was one of the most grueling fights in boxing history—a fight in which the two men tried to subdue not just each other, but also their desire to lie down and quit, just flat quit, out of a fatigue so complete it was mind-numbing. And who could have blamed them? The fight lasted 75 rounds— 75 rounds—a figure hard to grasp for a generation in which a 12-round bout qualifies as an epic match. It went on for two hours, 16 minutes and 23 seconds—an eternity for the men who endured the savagery on a day fit for the gate-keepers of hell.

In the 44th round, Sullivan began to vomit—the result, no doubt, of his drinking habits. Kilrain, seeing his chance for redemption, asked the champion, "Will you draw the fight?" And Sullivan, his belly still performing a rumba, roared back, "No, you loafer!" And so it went, for 10, 20, 30 more rounds. And then, in the 75th round, Sullivan fired a tremendous combination, his arms spinning like rotary blades, and Kilrain went down—a man beaten by the heat and the champion. Kilrain, slumped in his corner, refused to come out for the 76th round, and his handlers threw in the sponge.

The great John L. would never be so great again, his weaknesses exposed just as his hands were being covered—by gloves. He was 33 years old when he agreed to fight "Gentleman Jim" Corbett, who was as elegant as Sullivan was brutish, in 1892. The fight was waged under the Marquess of Queensberry rules, and Sullivan seemed lost—a pug matched against an artist. Corbett, a quick and clever fighter, outboxed the former bare-knuckle champion, helping to launch the era when boxing would become, once and for all, the "sweet science."

During the early 1900s, boxing remained illegal throughout most of the United States. Then in 1920, New York passed the Walker Law, which permitted public prizefighting—a huge breakthrough, considering that New York had hounded Sullivan less than 40 years earlier, forcing him to fight John Flood on a barge floating along the Hudson River. Those days of backroom brawling were over for good. In 1921, George "Tex" Rickard promoted the first match to draw a $1 million gate, the heavyweight championship bout between challenger Jack Dempsey and Frenchman Georges Carpentier on July 2, 1921, in Jersey City, New Jersey. The sport had arrived, legitimized by both fans and legislators, an astounding turn of events for a spectacle with such brutal origins and so rooted in the human tendency toward violence.

ABOVE: Above: By the early 1920s, professional boxing had become a full-blown sensation, as the impressive crowd for this July 2, 1921, fight between Jack Dempsey and Georges Carpentier shows. The first bout to attract a $1 million gate, it was billed as "The Battle of the Century." Alas, like so many overhyped contests before and since, the fight turned out to be something of a wash: Dempsey crushed his outclassed opponent in just the 4th round.

# THE FIGHTERS

No one looking at his countenance could fail to see that he was a fighting man by profession, and any judge of the fancy, considering his 6 feet in height, his 13 stone of solid muscle, and his beautifully graceful build, would admit that he had started his career with advantages which, if they were only backed by the driving power of a stout heart, must carry him far.

—Sir Arthur Conan Doyle, *The Lord of Falconbridge*

Fighters are prisoners of their bodies, their physiques the stone walls that trap them, that force them to fight in a certain style. Take Joe Frazier, the former heavyweight champion, for example. Frazier was short and squat, with a punch that could travel from his instep to your chin, and he fought with the fury of a scorned lover. He was a great fighter, not a great boxer, because he was not built for boxing; he was built for back-alley brawls. "I'll be a-smokin," he liked to say before his fights, describing his rough-and-tumble style. "Just like always." Frazier rarely threw the jab—one of the few great fighters in history who excluded that punch from his arsenal—but he boasted surprisingly good defense, his head bobbing with the frenetic motion of a speed bag. And he was so intimidating that George Foreman, who ended up defeating him for the heavyweight title, was terrified of him. "I was afraid of him," Foreman said. "I didn't want to fight him. I knew he loved to ride that motorcycle of his, and I was hoping he'd get into a crash and die before the fight. Frazier was mean, man, vicious. He could hit like a mule, but that wasn't the worst of it. You'd hit him, and he'd smile. Scary."

Muhammad Ali, who met his short, squat counterpart in three epic bouts, was different. Tall and sleek, with a spine that seemed to be made out of cartilage rather than bone, he was remarkably supple, able to bend his back to avoid punches that were all but certain to slam him—crunch—right in the jaw. Like all great boxers, Ali hated to get hit, so he maintained a zone, a distance, between himself and his opponent—a kind of force field that prevented him from getting rapped on the jaw. He did not mind taking shots to the belly—witness his open invitation to George Chuvalo, who hit him at will in the midsection on March 29, 1966, in Toronto—but the chin, well, that was another story. Ali did not want that. So he would dance from side to side, the ultimate moving target, always staying close enough to punch but far enough to keep from getting punched. It was a delicate balance, one that he maintained throughout much of his career. "Can't nobody beat me," Ali would scream. "I'm too pretty." He was a boxer.

Two fighters, two styles—one a raw, unpolished brawler, the other an elegant dancer. Why were they so different? They were limited by their bodies, although

OPPOSITE: Junior welterweight champion Julio Cesar Chavez celebrates his 2nd-round knockout of Scott Walker on February 9, 1996. ABOVE: One of the classic rivalries of boxing was between these two men, Jake LaMotta and Sugar Ray Robinson. Where Robinson was poetry in motion, the very embodiment of coordination and fluid power, LaMotta was stolid and sturdy, an earthbound, muscular fighter who was capable of weathering unbelievable abuse. Together they produced some of boxing's great match-ups.

their skills—and their hearts—allowed them to overcome whatever limitations their physiques imposed on their styles. And that is true not just of Ali and Frazier, but of every great fighter who has ever stepped into the ring. There is no blueprint, no outline, for greatness in this sport. A great fighter may be as coarse and unrefined as Jake LaMotta, the "Raging Bull," or as subtle and efficient as Julio Cesar Chavez, "el gran campeon Mexicano"—the great Mexican champion. Ultimately, great fighters share only two qualities: a fierce desire to win and the ability to achieve that win, with whatever style they choose—or whatever style their bodies choose for them.

## Jack Johnson

Proud and arrogant, a furious puncher, he should have been the hero, the darling, of the United States of America, just as John L. Sullivan had been a generation before. He boasted, after all, many of the traits that endeared the great John L. to the sporting public—he was smug and boastful, with a taste for both liquor and women. This janitor's son was also, throughout most of his career, unbeatable.

Born in Galveston, Texas, in 1878, Jack Johnson also happened to be black, and so, unlike John L. Sullivan, he was vilified, the target of a country that preferred its heroes white. The great John L. had refused to defend his title against black fighters, and the world applauded his decision. But Tommy Burns, then the world heavyweight champion, gave Johnson a shot, and Johnson made history, slamming white America in the gut with his victory.

Johnson proved that power and cunning could elevate a man above narrow thinking and within reach of the heavyweight title. Johnson, who stood 6 feet 1¼ inches (186cm) and weighed 192 pounds (87kg), was not just a great fighter; he was a superb boxer, his hand speed so startling that he seemed to be playing patty-cake with his opponents.

Johnson won the world heavyweight title on December 26, 1908, in Sydney, Australia, stopping Burns in the 14th round, and in the process becoming the first black man to rule the world with his fists—and, some hoped, the last. Johnson floored Burns with a peculiar punch: a right uppercut that he delivered

without pivoting, like one of those rock-'em-sock-'em robots that would hit toy stores several generations later. It was a punch that packed both fistic and social significance—Jack Johnson, black heavyweight champion. The racists came out of hiding, storming the fighter like ants attacking a picnic table. One of them was the great American adventure writer Jack London, who apparently reserved his love and sensitivity for wild dogs, not black heavyweight champions.

"The fight, if fight it must be called, was like that between a pigmy and a colossus," London, reporting from ringside for the *New York Herald*, wrote. "A dew drop had more of a chance than Burns with the giant Texan." London called for a former champion, James J. Jeffries, to come out of retirement and challenge the black title holder. "Remove that golden smile from Jack Johnson's face," London exhorted. Jeffries, who emerged from his alfalfa farm in California, challenged Johnson on July 4, 1910, in Reno, Nevada—the first of a procession of Great White Hopes. Johnson stopped him in the 15th round, conquering both his opponent and his racist supporters. But the racists would have their day. Age and fast living caught up to Johnson, and they were more brutal than any opponent he had faced in the ring.

Convicted of violating the Mann Act for transporting a white woman, Belle Schreiber, from Pittsburgh to Chicago for "immoral purposes" (a trumped-up charge using a statute created to stop organized crime), the champion jumped bail and fled to Europe in 1913. He continued to fight, successfully defending his title three times, but he conducted most of his "training" sessions at nightclubs in Paris, and he became slow and awkward.

On April 5, 1915, in Havana, Cuba, he fought Jess Willard, the latest in a series of white challengers. The promoter lured the champion by suggesting that federal authorities would consider a pardon if he lost the fight—a suggestion that would fuel speculation and debate for years to come. Willard floored the heavyweight king in the 26th round. Johnson, then 37, lay on the canvas for several minutes, shielding his eyes from the fierce sun—proof, skeptics suggested, that he

OPPOSITE: Two of the greatest fighters of the early 1900s, middleweight champion Stanley Ketchel (left) and heavyweight champion Jack Johnson (center), pose with boxing official Jim Coffrath before their bout on October 16, 1909, won by Johnson with a 12th-round knockout. Johnson added the middleweight crown to his collection with the win.

could have risen from the knockdown. Whether or not he took a dive, the former champion never got the pardon that the promoter had waved in his face. Johnson returned to the United States in 1920, serving nine months of his sentence at Leavenworth Penitentiary in Kansas. Johnson died in a car accident on June 10, 1946, in Raleigh, North Carolina. He was 68.

## Jack Dempsey and Gene Tunney

They were the Ali and Frazier of their era—the brawler and the boxer, inextricably linked by their two historic meetings. Jack Dempsey was the brawler, Gene Tunney the boxer, and as with all timeless pairings, their fights were great theater, providing so much drama that fans still discuss the matches generations later. And who could blame them? The fights were classics.

Tunney defeated Dempsey in both fights, and the country never forgave him. Dempsey was a hero or, more appropriately, an anti-hero—Babe Ruth with a scowl, a charismatic figure who enchanted the public with his fierce determination. He was the John L. Sullivan of his era, minus some of the vices, and captured the imagination of a country that still treasured toughness and individuality. Dempsey was a legend, and unlike most such figures, he did not have to retire before the status was bestowed upon him; he earned it during his career.

Born and raised in Manassa, Colorado, the ninth of thirteen children born to poor and hard-luck parents, William Harrison Dempsey left home in his teens, hopping freight trains and working in copper mines in Colorado and Utah. He toiled in the pits, and he chewed pine tar, a habit that strengthened his jaw against the assaults he would soon face in the ring. The ring? The world was his ring, at least in the beginning, because he stood up to the bullies and roughnecks in the mining camps, developing the reputation that would lead to his nickname, "the Manassa

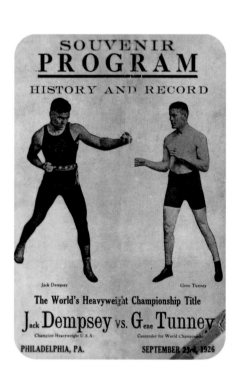

SOUVENIR
**PROGRAM**
HISTORY AND RECORD

*The World's Heavyweight Championship Title*
**J**ack **Dempsey** vs. **G**ene **Tunney**
Champion Heavyweight U.S.A.        Contender for World Championship
PHILADELPHIA, PA.                SEPTEMBER 23, 1926

Mauler." The teenager tired of working for pay and fighting for free, and he hit the freights again, this time stopping not at mining camps but at saloons, where he could fight for small purses. He adopted the name Jack after the great nineteenth-century lightweight—a name that he graced with his exploits in the ring. Dempsey destroyed Jess Willard, the erstwhile "Great White Hope," on July 4, 1919, in Toledo, Ohio, battering him so brutally that the Dempsey camp, according to legend, found a tooth embedded in one of his gloves. The fighting hobo was the new heavyweight champion, a popular but somewhat malignant presence on the boxing landscape. Sportswriters described his "concentrated cruelty," his "will to kill": "His body, muscled like a panther cat's, seems to ignite with malice, to burn and flash; then his fists reach out, savagely, lethally to destroy the weaving shape in front of him and get revenge for something he has just remembered, a wrong done, a score that must be evened, something that happened to him long ago," penned an awed writer in *Time* magazine.

Tunney was different. He was a delicate man in a savage sport—tall and handsome, with unmarked features that he wanted to keep unmarked. He was born in Greenwich Village, New York, the son of respectable working-class parents. Tunney was bright and articulate, often more so than the sportswriters who were forced to thumb through another play by Shakespeare or another novel by William Somerset Maugham to track down another quotation, another pearl of wisdom, from this most unusual of heavyweight prizefighters.

If he was gentle and articulate outside the ring, Tunney was remarkably dainty and composed inside the ring—an ideal foil for his opponent. This was not

ABOVE: A souvenir program proved amazingly prescient in its use of the word "history" to describe the first championship bout between Jack Dempsey and Gene Tunney, on September 23, 1926. It proved to be a fight for the ages, and was another illustration of technique versus determination where technique (that is, Tunney) carried the day. OPPOSITE: Heavyweight champion Jack Dempsey, looking as solid and noble as a Greek statue in this photograph, was feared and admired for his "killer instinct," but it was his incredible hand speed, wicked left hook, and high tolerance for pain that made him a truly lethal opponent.

In the infamous "long-count" episode of the rematch between Dempsey and Tunney, the Manassa Mauler stands in his corner as the referee counts over the fallen Tunney. Tunney went on to win this September 22, 1927, bout by decision, but the 4 extra seconds he got on the mat tarnished the victory, adding an asterisk to what otherwise was another tactical masterpiece.

"the Manassa Mauler," a bruiser who would accept five punches for the privilege of delivering one. No, Tunney was a clever and shifty boxer, as elusive as a wisp of smoke—the forerunner of such great heavyweights as Ali and Larry Holmes. He was the perfect challenger for Dempsey.

"Gene Shows He Has No Carbon in Ring Machinery," a *Chicago Tribune* headline trumpeted before the two men faced each other in the ring. They met for the first time on September 23, 1926, in Philadelphia—a long-anticipated match between two of the greatest heavyweights in the world. Tunney won a clear-cut decision, frustrating the champion with his superior boxing skills. But if Dempsey lost in one arena, he won in another, because the public would grow to love him more in defeat than it had in victory. The antihero had become a hero. "Honey," Dempsey explained to his wife, "I forgot to duck."

long count or no long count. Tunney went on to score another 10-round decision, but the long-count controversy persists to this day; right or wrong, it makes Dempsey shine more brightly than the man who defeated him, the gentle man in a savage sport.

## Joe Louis

Almost thirty years after Jack Johnson won the heavyweight title, another black champion emerged on the scene—Joe Louis. But this was a different time, a different America, and the nation embraced Louis as passionately as it had scorned Johnson. The warmer response was hardly surprising. Louis was a proud but humble man, more quiet and dignified than his predecessor, who had behaved in a way that was unacceptable to bigoted Americans. "The Brown Bomber," as Louis was called, once said that his opponents "can run, but they can't hide," and that seems as close as he ever came to boasting.

Not that Louis escaped racism. How could he? He was a black man in the 1930s. "The Brown Bomber"? As offensive as that nickname might be to contemporary society, it was one of the milder tags that sportswriters hung on the gifted champion. They also called him "the Shufflin' Shadow," "the Dusky Downer," "the Dark Destroyer," "the Sable Cyclone," and "the Coffee-Colored Kayo King."

"A physician who has observed Louis...compares the bomber to a primordial organism; says in temperament, he is like a one-celled beastie of the mire-and-steaming ooze period," Meyer Berger wrote in *The New York Times Magazine* in 1936. "Fighting, he displays boxing intelligence tantamount to the stalking instinct of the panther....He becomes sheer animal."

Physicians—or sportswriters—rarely described white fighters in such an ugly and offensive manner. But they failed to understand one thing about Louis: he was a powerful man, perhaps the greatest punching machine to ever step into the ring, his combinations short and sweet and solid. He was also ruthless in the ring, exhibiting the coldhearted brutality of a contract killer. But most great fighters are ruthless; it is, after all, an ugly sport, a sport in which inflicting punishment and inflicting it often are the primary goals. Louis was no different in that regard.

They fought again almost exactly a year later, on September 22, 1927, in Chicago, marking the first $2 million gate in boxing history. The challenger staggered Tunney with a right hand in the 7th round, following up with a combination that dropped the champion onto the seat of his white silk trunks. There was only one problem: Dempsey failed to retreat to a neutral corner following the knockdown, as the rules of the day clearly stated. The referee shoved Dempsey into a neutral corner, thus giving the champion extra time to recover from the knockdown, although it seems clear that Tunney could have risen before 10 seconds,

ABOVE: As stoic as he was powerful, Joe Louis barely smiles as announcer Hal Totten raises the champ's arm in the aftermath of the Brown Bomber's crushing knockout of James J. Braddock on June 22, 1937. Embracing Louis is his manager, Julius Black. It was a stunning comeback: one year before Louis won the heavyweight championship from Braddock, the Bomber had been delivered his first beating, at the hands of Max Schmeling. OPPOSITE: On June 22, 1938—a year to the day after taking the heavyweight title from James Braddock—champion Joe Louis avenged his demoralizing loss to Max Schmeling by felling the German in the first round of the rematch. Here, Louis daintily steps back as he surveys what 124 seconds of pummeling has done to his opponent.

What truly set Louis apart from other boxers of the day—and what the racists failed to recognize—was that he was perhaps the smartest fighter of his generation, a man who never made the same mistake twice. Never. Louis was not the dancer—or the showman— that Ali would be, but he was a tremendous boxer, a model of economy and precision. He could flatten you with punches that traveled only 5 inches (13cm). Louis an animal? Hardly. He was a gifted, intelligent boxer, a man who, despite the racism of his day, became a

national hero as socially significant as Jackie Robinson, who would break the color barrier in major league baseball a generation later. Louis "was a tremendous puncher, with tremendous hand speed, and he never wasted movement," said trainer Eddie Futch, his boyhood friend.

If Louis became "a black hero in white America"— the title of the brilliant biography by Chris Mead—it was because of his two battles with the German fighter Max Schmeling. Schmeling became a symbol of Nazi

Germany, particularly during the second fight, and while some historians feel the label was unfair, it did not seem to matter. History is an overwhelming force, carrying with it a tidal wave of emotions and sentiments, and to fans in the United States, Schmeling was Nazi Germany.

Schmeling shocked the American, then an up-and-comer, on June 19, 1936, in New York, knocking him out in the 12th round. The German had detected a weakness in Louis, a weakness that the sportswriters, in all their wisdom, had failed to notice. Whenever the American threw the jab, he dropped his left, thus leaving him open to right-hand counters. Schmeling battered Louis throughout the bout, but the final combination was the most brutal of the fight: two right hands to the jaw—the first an uppercut, the second a chopping blow. The American fell into the ropes, both of his arms hanging over the middle strands, where he remained so motionless that he looked like a subject for

a still life. The invincible warrior finally crumpled onto the canvas. "All you have to do to beat him is walk into him and bang him with a solid punch," Jack Dempsey, the former champion, said of Louis. "I don't think he'll ever whip another good fighter."

Dempsey was wrong. Louis and Schmeling fought again on January 22, 1938, at Yankee Stadium in New York, but this was a different Louis. He had committed a disastrous error in the first fight, dropping his left after firing the jab, and he had corrected that mistake in training—a mistake he would never repeat. The American also entered the ring as heavyweight champion, having won the title with an 8th-round knockout of Jimmy Braddock less than a year earlier in Chicago. When asked if he was nervous heading into the fight, Louis responded, "Yeah, I'm afraid that I might kill Schmeling tonight."

With all the confidence that comes with winning the title, Louis climbed into the ring against the symbol of Nazi Germany. Louis destroyed him. He pinned Schmeling against the ropes, and the challenger looked like a flounder in a net, writhing helplessly against the assault. Louis pounded him relentlessly, each punch

landing on the ribs with a sickening thud. The challenger fell to the canvas, his ribs broken, the vision of Nazi Germany shattered. The fight had lasted 124 seconds. Louis, already a hero to black America, became a hero to all of America. "He's a credit to his race—the human race," Jimmy Cannon wrote. The rest of the nation was just as proud, just as effusive. "Louis has finally come into his full estate as a great world's champion," wrote Dan Parker of the *New York Daily Mirror*. "If anyone doubts his greatness after his masterful job last night, he's plain plumb prejudiced."

Louis retired after World War II, only to return two years later, but his skills were as faded as his press clippings. He lost a heavyweight title bid to Ezzard Charles, who had won the championship on

September 9, 1950, in New York. Then, in one of the saddest spectacles in boxing history, he fought a young up-and-comer, Rocky Marciano, who knocked out the former champion on October 26, 1951, in New York—the last battle of a great warrior and an even greater human being.

## Sugar Ray Robinson

The great boxing historian Pierce Egan may have coined the term "the sweet science" in 1824, but it took Walker Smith to give the phrase substance and credibility more than one hundred years later. Walker Smith? You might know him better as Sugar Ray Robinson, perhaps the greatest fighter who ever lived—a status that *Ring Magazine* bestowed upon him in 1997. Fans still marvel at his artistry. He threw combinations that had never been seen before or since—firing hooks off uppercuts and uppercuts off hooks, usually with a dizzying speed that rendered his superb defense unnecessary. After all, who could counter a hailstorm of punches to the body and head?

"He was the greatest fighter of all time," Ali said. "I styled my dancing moves after him. He had a hard, hard punch and could back up and dance. He was a pretty fighter with excellent rhythm." Great stylists began to emerge after the turn of the century—fighters such as heavyweight champion Jack Johnson, lightweight champion Benny Leonard, and featherweight champion Kid Chocolate. They bobbed and weaved, feinted and counterpunched, jabbed and crossed over with the right—tactics that, though common today, were considered revolutionary in the bare-knuckle days. The stylists pushed boxing, step by step, punch by punch, into the twentieth century.

"There were great fighters before Robinson, but it was Robinson who put everything together in one package—speed, grace, power," said Eddie Futch, the great former trainer who guided more than fifteen fighters to world titles during his career. "If you look at some of the boxers Robinson fought—Jake LaMotta, Gene Fullmer, Carmen Basilio—you see a clear contrast in styles. They were the awkward brawlers. He was the artist."

Ali was not the only boxer who copied that sweet, graceful style. Robinson altered boxing just as surely

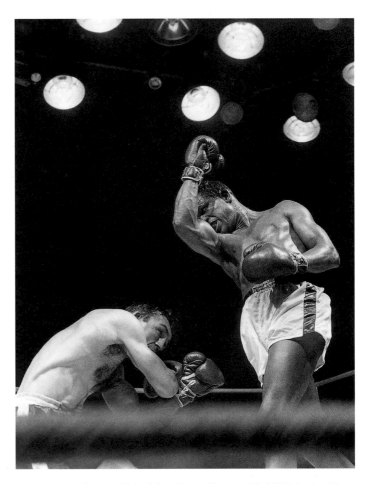

OPPOSITE: Bending so low his head almost touches the canvas, Jake LaMotta barely avoids the dazzlingly quick blows of Sugar Ray Robinson on Valentine's Day, 1951. Robinson won this fight, the last of their classic rivalry, and in the process secured the middleweight crown.
ABOVE: Sugar Ray Robinson, heroically ignoring the ill effects of a 103-degree fever caused by a viral infection, scored a 15th-round decision over Carmen Basilio in this middleweight title fight on March 25, 1958.

as he altered the nervous systems of his opponents—perhaps with the same disastrous results. Why? Because there was only one Sugar Ray Robinson, and while Ali and Sugar Ray Leonard were successful imitators, most fighters were pathetic copycats. They showed good taste, not good judgment, in copying a legend. In the end, these clones were miserable failures.

"If anyone has come along since to equal Sugar Ray Robinson, I don't know who it has been," Futch said. "Muhammad Ali was a great boxer—a great boxer—the nearest thing to Sugar Ray Robinson. But Robinson could do things that Ali couldn't. Ali didn't have that one-punch knockout power that Robinson did. Ali went 41 rounds with Joe Frazier and never once put him down.

"Sugar Ray Robinson represented the finest qualities you can find in a boxer—his style, his class, his grace and his consummate artistry. He could box, and he could punch. You wouldn't expect a ballet dancer to be able to kill you with one punch, but Robinson could."

One man who discovered that painful truth was Artie Levine, a top contender whom Robinson knocked out in the 10th round on November 6, 1946, in Cleveland. "Robinson caught Levine with a shot to the chin," Futch recalled. "Levine backed into the ropes, and Robinson started raining punches on him. Levine had his arms up, and he was blocking everything Robinson threw. Robinson noticed the body was open. He threw a right to the body, and Levine went down. The referee counted him out." After the fight, Futch went to the dressing room, where one of his boxers was preparing for the walkout bout. "Levine came in, and he was upset," Futch said. "I asked him, 'What's up?' He said, 'That was a fast count. The ref just said 10, and that was it.' I had to explain that 10 was the last number the referee had counted, not the first. The poor man had been out cold."

Robinson was so quick that he could get away with an illegal punch—a left hook that snaked around the body and landed on the small of the back. Imagine a nightstick jammed into the base of your spine. "That punch paralyzed his opponents," said George Benton, a former middleweight contender who trained ten world champions. "Referees never saw it because it came so quickly." Benton, a native of Philadelphia, had firsthand knowledge of that punch. "I remember once, when I was 15 years old. I was an amateur, boxing in New York. I was fighting this older kid who had been training in Sugar Ray's gym. The kid had picked up that left hook from Robinson. He hit me with it, and it took my legs away. I lost the decision. It was an education."

From 1940 to 1964, Robinson compiled a professional record of 175-19-6, including 110 knockouts. Eighteen of those losses came after he was 30. His only loss before that point was to LaMotta on February 5, 1943—the only fight LaMotta won in six meetings with Robinson. "You know why Jake LaMotta did so well against him?" Benton asked. "Because LaMotta had a great chin, and because he was half-nuts. I don't mean insane. But LaMotta had no fear, and a person without fear has to be a little crazy. How else can you explain all those punches he took from Robinson?" How do you explain it? You cannot explain it any more than you can explain how Robinson threw them in the first place, how he threw the most beautiful combinations in boxing history.

## Henry Armstrong

Henry Armstrong was a whirlwind, his fists flashing out of a vortex that seemed impossible to defend. Of all his attributes—and he had many—the single most important was his energy. He was like a sprinter in a long-distance race who churned furiously while his opponents loped steadily. There was no feeling-out process for Armstrong, no taking a round off to size up his opponent. No, his feeling-out process came before the fight, in the dressing room, where he would work out feverishly. Not warm up—work out, speed bag and all. Armstrong had to release some of that energy and tension before the fight; otherwise, he would be a maniac, his punches spraying like machine-gun fire, during the fight.

Born Henry Jackson on December 12, 1912, in Columbus, Missouri, he was one of fifteen children whose father worked as a farmer and butcher. As a teenager during the Depression, he worked for the Missouri-Pacific Railroad, but one day he saw a newspaper headline that served as a giant recruitment poster—a recruitment poster for prizefighting. The headline stated, "Kid Chocolate Earns $75,000 For Half-Hour's Work." That was the only vocational guidance the young man needed. He quit his job, telling his buddies, "I'm coming back in a Cadillac."

Changing his name to Armstrong, a tribute to a former fighter named Harry Armstrong, he almost came back in an ambulance, not a Cadillac, because his dream met with disaster in his professional debut on July 27, 1931. He was knocked out in the 3rd round by Al Iovino, a southpaw. But the young man picked himself—and his career—off the canvas, developing the frenetic style that would help offset his short stature. Armstrong stood only 5 feet 5 1/2 inches (166cm), but he punched so furiously that his short reach became an asset, turning a disadvantage into an advantage with his punishing inside fighting. The sportswriters called him "Hammerin' Hank."

Bobbing, weaving, and punching his way through the division, Armstrong won his first world title on October 29, 1937, with a 6th-round knockout over featherweight king Petey Sarron. But the featherweight division was not enough, not for a man as talented and ambitious as Armstrong. Next? He jumped to the wel-

Adding the lightweight title to his welterweight and featherweight crowns with the win, Henry "Hurricane Hank" Armstrong celebrates his 15-round decision over Lou Ambers on August 17, 1938. The campaign to win all three world titles was waged partly out of financial considerations, and partly to get attention: given the boxing world's fixation with heavyweight Joe Louis, there was little notice paid to such chicken-legged lightweights as Armstrong. But the brain trust backing Armstrong—which included Hollywood luminaries George Raft and Al Jolson—decided that "Hammerin' Hank" (as he was also known), with his unbelievable energy and stamina, could pull off the trifecta. They were right. Hank Armstrong won all three world titles in just more than nine months, making good money in the process and proving that he was one of the very best boxers to fight in any weight class ever.

terweight division, a leap of about 20 pounds (9kg) that he executed easily, if not wisely. How did he do it? He trained on beer. Armstrong would not revolutionize training routines with his curious regimen, but it was successful. He pounded welterweight champion Barney Ross on May 31, 1938, in New York, scoring a unanimous decision to win his second world title in less than a year.

With two title belts cinched around his waist, Armstrong yearned to expand his wardrobe—with, yes, another championship belt. This time he went down to the lightweight division—the weight class between featherweight and welterweight—to challenge Lou Ambers, the world champion who was one of the classiest stylists of his era. It would prove one of the toughest bouts in the careers of both men. Fighting with a torn lip that forced him to swallow his own blood for the last 5 rounds, Armstrong faced three opponents—nausea, fatigue, and Ambers. But he hung on; somehow, he hung on, capturing a split decision in a brutal, grueling 15-round match. Armstrong won the lightweight title only ten weeks after defeating Ross, making it three world titles in less than a year—a sensational achievement that no other fighter has ever matched.

After winning the lightweight title, Armstrong relinquished the first crown he won—the featherweight

title. Then he made what turned out to be his only
lightweight defense: losing a decision to Ambers after
being penalized 5 rounds for punching low. Two titles
won, two titles gone. Ah, but it was the third division,
the welterweight division, in which Armstrong left his
mark. He defended the welterweight title an astounding
nineteen times, including eleven in one year—1939.
The streak ended when Fritzie Zivic outpointed him on
January 17, 1941.

## Willie Pep

They called him "the Will-o'-the-Wisp," and he turned
his matches into exhibitions that boasted all the dread
and menace of a pillow fight. This was not prizefighting; this was, well, boxing. And Willie Pep was one of
the greatest boxers who ever lived, a guy who could go
entire rounds without getting breathed on, much less
pounded on. Was his style exciting? It depended on
how much artistry you wanted to see in your pugs. If
you preferred mayhem over craft, Pep was not your
guy, and he was not the guy for some of the sportswriters of his day. He outpointed Chalky Wright for
the world featherweight title on November 20, 1942,
in New York, and the pundits were not pleased. "Pep
retreated faster and more frequently than Rommel's
Afrika Corps," wrote Dick McCann of the New York
*Daily News*. Columnist Frank Graham was even more
brutal: "There is, in short, nothing to distinguish Pep
from a dozen other featherweights." Wrong. Pep was
special. He could not punch hard, but since he was not
getting punched in return, it was not a critical deficit.
Pep held the featherweight title for seven years, off and
on, and he compiled an amazing record of 229-11-1,
with sixty-five knockouts, from 1940 to 1966. The
smart sportswriters saw the real thing in Pep. "Pep
was the greatest creative artist I ever saw in a ring,"
wrote the great sportswriter W.C. Heinz in 1979. "Pep
was a poet, often implying, with his feints and his footwork, more than he said."

RIGHT: Featherweight great Willie Pep, his face bleeding from 15 rounds of punishment,
celebrates a dramatic victory by decision over Sandy Saddler on February 11, 1949, at Madison
Square Garden. The Fred Astaire of the ring, Pep was a defensive specialist who more than made
up for his lack of power with dazzling footwork and beguiling feints. Making the comeback victory
over the taller, stronger Saddler even more remarkable was the fact that this was the second
stage of Pep's career; the first had been brought to a close by a January 8, 1947, airplane crash
that had left Pep with life-threatening injuries. Five months later, Pep was not only on his feet
but in the ring.

Pep was absurdly dominant—135-1-1, with a five-year unbeaten streak—until he met Sandy Saddler on October 29, 1948, in New York. The champion was short and clever, while the challenger was tall and powerful, one of the most bruising punchers the division had ever seen. Pep was a three-to-one favorite, but the favorite looked like an underdog the moment the bell rang. Saddler crushed Pep in the 4th round, turning "the Will-o'-the-Wisp" into a fencing dummy in short pants, stationary and vulnerable. Pep won the rematch three months later, surviving cuts above both eyes to regain his title with a unanimous decision. The creative genius overcame the puncher, but Pep had lost his defensive mastery against his most worthy opponent, finishing the bout with bruises all over his face. They fought two more times, with Pep losing both of the battles, the most brutal being the third fight in their classic series. Pep and Saddler looked like the ancestors of Roberto Duran—one of the dirtiest fighters of the 1970s, '80s, and '90s—grabbing, pushing, and thumbing each other in the eyes. They locked bodies in the 7th round, becoming one amorphous mass with four arms, four legs, and two fighting hearts. Pep returned to his corner, complaining about a pain that was later diagnosed as a dislocated shoulder. The bell rang for the 8th round, but Pep, ahead on all three cards, remained on his stool, and Saddler won the fight. "He beat me with a double arm-lock," Pep said, moaning after the fight. Saddler disagreed. "I thought a punch to the kidney did it," he said. "But if they say I twisted his arm, okay, I twisted it."

## Rocky Marciano

It was a thunderclap of a punch, and it landed where every great punch should land—in our collective consciousness. If you were at the fight, or if you have seen the famous photograph of the punch, you will never forget it. It is not a pretty picture, but it is a classic one: Rocky Marciano catching Jersey Joe Walcott on the jaw—188 pounds (85kg) of force concentrated in one leather glove. Marciano won the heavyweight title with that punch—a right hand that turned Walcott into an ugly caricature of himself, his features suddenly distorted, his ears where his cheeks should have been, his mouth where his nose should have been, his eyes so

blank that he looked like a dead fish. It was horrible, and boxing fans will remember it forever.

Marciano delivered that right hand on September 23, 1952, in Philadelphia, and it seemed to cement his status as a legend-in-the-making. Why? Because it was not merely an awesome punch; it was an awesome punch that came when Marciano needed it most. Behind on points, his nose broken from the relentless attack of a man almost eleven years older, Marciano needed a miracle to win the fight—and he got it. Marciano knocked out Walcott in the 13th round and captured the heavyweight title that Walcott had seemed certain to retain.

"The Brockton Blockbuster" went on to win six more fights, including a surprisingly easy rematch over Walcott and two classic battles with Ezzard Charles, a clever boxer and a solid puncher. He also won a fight without having to land a single blow—the computer fight with Muhammad Ali in 1969. Experts fed information on each boxer into the computer, including strengths and weaknesses, and the computer spit out the result. Ali and Marciano acted out the result in a ring in a film studio. Fans, not knowing the outcome of this computer matchup, witnessed the contrived battle as if it were a real fight. It was not, and boxing experts

ABOVE: Rocky Marciano and trainer Charlie Goldman discuss strategy during training camp for the champ's title defense against Roland La Starza on September 24, 1953. As always, Marciano won, on this occasion with an 11th-round knockout at New York's Polo Grounds. Amazingly, Marciano had the shortest reach among all heavyweight champions.

ABOVE: Rocky Marciano slams his signature right into the jaw of Jersey Joe Walcott on September 23, 1952, one of the most famous punches in boxing history. Born Rocco Francis Marchegiano, Marciano began his pro career in 1947 with a knockout of Lee Epperson. Before his next fight, almost a year and a half later, the raw, awkward Marciano had put in serious time studying the sweet science with legendary trainer Charlie Goldman. Goldman tinkered with everything about Marciano's game except one: his right power punch. Goldman called it the "Suzy-Q" and it sure came in handy throughout Marciano's romp through the heavyweight division.

will tell you why: because Marciano won. For all of his toughness, for all of his determination and will power, Rocky Marciano was no Muhammad Ali. But it was a testament to his character and his reputation that somebody, even if it was a computer, thought he could beat the great Ali.

Marciano retired in 1956, having won forty-nine fights, forty-three of them by knockout—the only champion in any weight class to retire undefeated. He threw thousands of punches in his career, from Connecticut to California, sometimes landing more blows in a round than some fighters did in entire fights.

But of all the punches he delivered, of all the jabs and hooks and crosses, none was more famous than the one he threw on the night of September 23, 1952.

## Archie Moore

They put on a fight, and an antique show broke out. Archie Moore scored a unanimous decision over Joey Maxim on December 17, 1952, in St. Louis, capturing the light heavyweight title with a brilliant display of boxing. It was a special moment—not just because Moore was gifted, but because he was gifted and old. He was 36, or 39, depending on who you asked, and Maxim was only 30. But age did not seem to matter to Moore. He fought with the passion and enthusiasm of a man half his age. Maxim found that out, and so did dozens of other fighters throughout the years. Years? Try decades. Moore fought from 1936 to 1963, compiling an astounding record of 194–26–8, with 141 of the wins coming by knockout.

If Moore fought long past the age when most fighters would have retired, there was a good reason for it. Moore wanted a title, and nobody would give him a shot at one. Moore had fought for sixteen years, ten of them as a contender, before Maxim finally gave him the opportunity he deserved. "I made up in fifteen rounds what I had missed in sixteen years," Moore said.

And it soon became clear why all the other champions had ducked Moore throughout his career. He was a terror, as clever as he was powerful—a man who could befuddle you with his defense and flatten you with his offense. Moore was a boxer-puncher. He may have been a complete fighter, but it was his defense that seemed so remarkable. The aging champion called it "escapology," the art of making your opponent think you are here when you are actually over there. Moore did it with superior upper body movement, his arms

crossed in front of him in case a punch strayed too close. He was so clever and shifty that one sportswriter dubbed him "the Mongoose."

"Escapology" failed "the Mongoose" on December 10, 1958, in Montreal. Moore was 44 years old, and for one night at least, he looked every year of it. The contender, Yvon Durelle, a crude and aggressive fighter from Canada, dropped the champion three times in the 1st round and once in the 5th, hammering him so brutally that the old man, dazed and disoriented, stumbled across the ring for much of the fight. Then something remarkable happened. The old man began to rally—the champion floored Durelle in the 7th, the 10th and, for the 10-count, the 11th. "The Mongoose" escaped again, coming back to knock the same man out in the 3rd round less than a year later.

After the Durelle rematch, Moore fought for four more years, including a match against Muhammad Ali, who said he was embarrassed to fight someone on Social Security. Moore retired in 1963, but if boxing missed the old man, it would not miss him forever. The ex-champion returned in 1987, not as a fighter but as a training consultant. And whom did he train but another ageless wonder, George Foreman. Foreman came back from a ten-year retirement to knock out Michael Moorer on November 5, 1994, and become the oldest heavyweight champion in boxing history—45 years old. "He's a wise man, and he can teach me a lot," Foreman said.

And so he did.

ABOVE: Archie Moore, the ageless marvel whose career spanned three decades, backs up challenger Joey Maxim on January 27, 1954. It was Moore's third match with the man from whom he had grabbed the light heavyweight title (on December 17, 1952). Moore won all three fights with Maxim. OPPOSITE: Archie Moore ducks low to avoid the blows of his opponent, Giulio Rinaldi of Italy, during the 12th round of their 15-round June 10, 1961, match-up. Though somewhere in his late forties at the time, Moore successfully defended his light heavyweight championship title, winning the fight by decision. Moore, also known as "the Mongoose," has the best knockout total in history: he sent more than 140 challengers to the mat over the course of his remarkable, and remarkably long, career.

## Muhammad Ali

The debate will rage for as long as men lace on a pair of gloves to whack each other in the ring: who was the greatest fighter who ever lived? Sugar Ray Robinson or Muhammad Ali? In the end the question, while intriguing, is pointless. Like van Gogh and Picasso, Ali and Robinson were different artists working in different genres—the former a heavyweight, the latter a welterweight and middleweight. Who was the best? It is impossible to answer that question without losing sleep over it. But one thing is clear. Like van Gogh and Picasso, Ali and Robinson were startling, almost breathtaking originals—showmen who could dazzle you the moment they stepped into the ring, as creative as they were brutal.

Ali was tall and pretty, and in his prime, when his talent matched his audacity, he could fire his combinations faster than the camera crew could shoot them, leaving a trail of opponents sprawled on the canvas with no photographic evidence—punch, punch, punch, click—of what put them there. He was amazing, and he did it all as a heavyweight, a weight class filled with pachyderms, which made his achievement all the more remarkable. Ali weighed about 215 pounds (98kg), at least 60 pounds (27kg) more than Robinson, but he was

ABOVE: The brash, rhyme-slinging Cassius Clay answers questions during a press conference while legendary trainer Angelo Dundee (standing far right) looks on. RIGHT: Muhammad Ali towers defiantly over the fallen Sonny Liston and taunts him, daring him to get up from the mat. Ali won this May 25, 1965, rematch by 1st-round knockout. After their first clash more than a year earlier, which Ali won in the 7th by TKO, Cassius Marcellus Clay was reborn as Muhammad Ali.

a featherweight—smooth and fast and graceful—until he stepped on the scale. But he could punch—and boast—like a heavyweight.

> This colorful fighter is something to see
> And the greatest heavyweight champion
> I know he will be
> —Muhammad Ali

Unlike Robinson, who was a model of precision, Ali did everything wrong. He never learned how to box—not in the conventional sense, anyway—but he created a unique style, and he had the athletic ability to overcome his mechanical flaws. "He was a very limited fighter," said Eddie Futch, who trained the greatest rival Ali ever faced, Joe Frazier. "But what he did, he did extremely well."

Ali won the heavyweight title on February 25, 1964, in Miami Beach, Florida, scoring a stunning knockout over Sonny Liston in one of the biggest upsets in boxing history. He won it again ten years later, with his reflexes and timing—but not his heart and wit—vastly inferior during his comeback. He defeated George Foreman, again with a stunning knockout, to regain the title. "The Greatest" would not stop there. Ali lost the title and regained it one more time, with both the defeat and the victory coming against Leon Spinks in 1978. At that time, he was the only man to win the heavyweight title three times, a feat since matched by Evander Holyfield. And he did it during perhaps the greatest era for heavyweights in boxing history. He fought Liston, Frazier, Archie Moore, George Foreman, Floyd Patterson, Jerry Quarry, Jimmy Ellis, Ken Norton, Ron Lyle, Earnie Shavers, Larry Holmes, and Bob Foster.

"He is the Prince of Heaven," Norman Mailer wrote in his book *The Fight*, repeating the kind of hyperbole that Ali inspired—and often expressed—throughout his career. But Mailer was not alone in his

praise. "He was a great, great, great fighter," said George Benton, an assistant trainer under Futch during the 1970s. "And as vicious as he could be inside the ring, that's how sweet he was outside the ring. He wouldn't hurt a fly." That is something that Frazier never understood.

Ali and Frazier fought in three memorable wars, the final battle being the legendary "Thrilla in Manila" on October 1, 1975. Futch stopped the fight after the 14th round, with Frazier protesting on his stool, his eyes closed by 42 minutes of punishment. Ali collapsed after the bout, his heart having kept him up long after

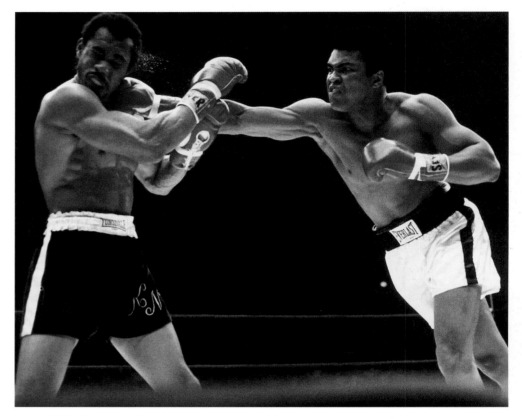

his legs wanted him to go down. "This is the closest thing to death there is," he said after the fight. The two men should have been bonded by those three battles, respect replacing the hostility they felt in the ring. But Ali taunted Frazier in and out of the ring, sometimes mercilessly, and Frazier, a proud man, had a difficult time forgetting and forgiving. "It's sad," Benton said. "Ali never meant the things he said to Frazier. But he was a businessman and a boxer, and he was just trying

ABOVE: Ali uses his long reach to rocket his right glove into the face of Ken Norton during one of their two fights in 1973. On the comeback trail in 1973, Ali first met Norton in March of that year and got the worst of the encounter: losing the fight and suffering a broken jaw for his efforts. Six months later, however, the glove was on the other fist: Ali stopped Norton, paving the way for the storied match-up against George Foreman in Kinshasa, Zaire, in 1974. OPPOSITE: Muhammad Ali rocks George Foreman with a straight right during their legendary "Rumble in the Jungle" on October 30, 1974.

# A Closer Look

Muhammad Ali, a biblical scholar in short pants, grabbed Joe Frazier in the middle of the ring. "I'm God," Ali told him.

Frazier—a fighter, not a scholar—was taken aback, but only momentarily. "What?" Frazier asked.

"I'm God," Ali repeated.

"Well, then, God's gonna get whupped tonight," Frazier said.

Frazier did whup Ali, not God, on March 8, 1971, in Madison Square Garden—the first of their three classic meetings. But if Ali proved mortal in the ring, he was still a titanic figure—loud and brash and talented. Even today, without his trunks, tassels, and gloves, Muhammad Ali could never be like the rest of us; he could never be ordinary. We thought the ring was his stage, but we were wrong; the world was his stage. And he commanded it with a presence that few people—athletes or politicians or entertainers—could match. He once knocked out the Beatles, all four of them, with a single punch. Sure, it was a publicity stunt, in a grimy old gym in Miami, but it seemed appropriate—the five greatest entertainers in the world going toe-to-toe. The Beatles sang "Love Me Do," while Ali recited "Me. We!" but both the Beatles and Ali were about ambition, about attaining heights that most men could not see, much less negotiate.

Who was this man, this enigma? Was he an actor? No, but he generated more drama than a troupe of Broadway stars. Was he a magician? No, but his hands were so fast that slow-motion cameras sometimes failed to pick up his punches. Was he a politician? No, but he could be more eloquent and impassioned than those who were. So who was this man? He was the greatest fighter—some might say the greatest figure—of his generation, and he remains a charismatic individual to this day.

Ali now suffers from Parkinson's disease, a chronic condition of the nervous system. The sickness forces him to walk slowly and speak haltingly, as if he were considering every word and measuring it for its impact upon the listener—a seemingly preposterous notion. After all, Ali never cared what his audience thought. Or did he? Oh, he cared all right, because the more outrageous the comment, the more satisfaction he got out of the reaction to it. The one thing Ali could not stand was indifference, and it was the one response he never got. People either loved him or hated him, although more and more people love Ali today. He has become an almost mythical figure, his stature growing stronger even as his body grows weaker.

It would be easy to pity this man, once so dynamic, now so frail. But it seems wrong to feel sorry for him. Why? It seems wrong to pity a man who refuses to pity himself. Ali never expected pity as a fighter, and he does not expect it as a man.

After losing to Frazier, then the heavyweight champion of the world, in their first fight, Ali sat in a wheelchair in a hospital corridor, his jaw swollen to the size of a grapefruit. A reporter told him that people were saying he did not want a rematch with Frazier. Ali looked at him for a second. "Oh, how wrong they are," he said quietly. "How wrong they are." *Sports Illustrated* later splashed across its cover the headline "End of the Ali Legend." The end? Hardly. It was the beginning, and the legend had as much to do with Ali the man as with Ali the fighter. "What I suffered physically was worth what I've accomplished in life," Ali said at a news conference to discuss his health in 1984. "A man who is not courageous enough to take risks will never accomplish anything in life." *Sports Illusrated* later came to the same conclusion, voting him athlete of the century in 1999.

Today, Ali lives on a farm in Berrien Springs, Michigan, with his fourth wife, Lonnie. He still punches the heavy bag, and he walks several miles every morning when his schedule allows. The ex–heavyweight champion travels widely to preach the religion of Islam, which he embraced more than thirty years ago, when he changed his name from Cassius Clay to Muhammad Ali. "It's the God in me that people connect with," Ali once said, explaining his hold on people.

No, he was not God, despite the assertion to Frazier on that night almost thirty years ago. But he was godlike, a deeply spiritual man who could be as caring outside the ring as he was vicious inside the ring. Ali seemed to rule the world in and out of the ring. What makes this man truly special is that more than any other athlete in history—more than Jack Johnson, more than Joe Louis, even more than Jackie Robinson—he has made the public look upon athletes as human beings, as people who could embody their eras as much as kings and statesmen did. "My name is known in Serbia, Pakistan, Morocco," he once said. "These are countries that don't follow the Kentucky Derby." Ali claimed he was more famous than the Pope. "And I don't have to wear one of those funny hats," he said.

For all his dazzling skills in the ring, however, Ali crossed over from athlete to social phenomenon because of the one battle he refused to wage—in Vietnam. "I got no quarrel with them Viet Cong," he said on February 17, 1966, when he refused induction into the armed services.

When Ali carried the torch for the 1996 Olympics in Atlanta, the world rejoiced. He walked slowly, the once magnificent Ali shuffle reduced to a slow, halting gait, and his hand trembling from the weight of the torch. But one thing remained as bright and vibrant as ever: his smile, sometimes mischievous, sometimes beatific. It was a wonderful moment.

Some fighters remain champions forever. Ali is one of them.

OPPOSITE: One of the most stirring sights in Olympic history occurred at the start of the 1996 Summer Olympics, when former Olympian Muhammad Ali—by then much afflicted by Parkinson's disease—mounted the stage and lit the device that in turn set the Olympic Cauldron aflame.

to drum up interest in their fights." Ali succeeded in doing just that: the fights comprised perhaps the greatest trilogy in boxing history. "Ali and Frazier were great fighters, anyway," boxing historian Bert Sugar said. "But they made each other greater."

## Roberto Duran

Geography meant nothing to Roberto Duran. No matter where he traveled, no matter where he fought, in New York or Las Vegas or Panama City, the streets were always with him—the streets of his youth, where fighting was more than a pugilistic exercise; it was a way of life. And Duran accepted it, mentally remaining on those streets even when his million-dollar paychecks told him to run, to flee, to get as far away from his past as possible. Not that Duran lived on the streets, mind you; he just took the streets with him wherever he went, especially into the ring, where he was one of the most artfully dirty fighters to ever thumb an opponent in the eye. A dirty fighter artful? Yeah, because his dirty tactics were subtle—or as subtle as dirty tactics can be in this brutal sport. If he missed a punch, for example, it did not matter, because he might catch you with his elbow in his follow-through. And if he landed the punch—well, that was worse, because he might catch you with his elbow anyway just for good measure. And his head was a third fist; he did not bother to glove it, but it was a fist.

Duran grew up in Panama City, Panama, shining shoes, peddling mangoes, and dancing in saloons. He also played the drums, and he might have become an accomplished musician, the star of his high school band, except for one thing—he discovered that he liked pounding people more than percussion instruments. Duran quit school in the third grade, his education moving to a less elegant academic forum—the streets. He was a star pupil, acquiring the only certificate of honor that means anything in the back alley: a reputation. Oh, yes, he had a reputation. Duran once dropped a horse with a single blow, according to legend, and whether the story was true or not, it should have been true. The legend of "Manos de Piedra"—"Hands of Stone"—was born.

Handlers rush to congratulate Roberto Duran, a legend in the making, after his devastating knockout of Scottish lightweight champion Ken Buchanan on June 26, 1972. The hard-hitting street fighter from the barrios of Panama City had come a long way from shining shoes for a pittance.

If Duran was a street fighter, he was a street fighter with class, a man whose punching power overshadowed his remarkable boxing ability. At first he fought for pocket change, the purses only slightly higher than the money he had earned peddling mangoes, but his earning power—and his reputation—grew. The young fighter fulfilled a dream on September 13, 1971, when

chalk outline around his body and started dusting for glove-prints. Huertas was out for six minutes. The fraud had proven himself.

The fans grew to love him, not just for his boxing ability but for the fierceness and menace with which he displayed it. Here was a man who loved only one thing more than beating people up—humiliating them after

ABOVE: Roberto Duran (left) stuns Carlos Palomino in the 4th round with a left hook during this June 22, 1979, welterweight bout at Madison Square Garden. Both fighters went the distance, but Duran won the fight by decision.

he fought in the mecca of boxing, Madison Square Garden. The fans saw a nobody, a skinny pug with ribs that threatened to burst through his skin. They derided him, seeing a fraud in short pants—a sensation in Panama, perhaps, but not in the United States. They were wrong. Duran knocked out Benny Huertas that day, leaving him so motionless, so deathly motionless, that in another setting the cops could have drawn a

he beat them up. He destroyed Carlos Palomino, once a tremendous fighter, on June 22, 1979, in New York, snarling afterward, "Quit. You don't got it no more." But that was kind and generous compared to what he had told Ray Lampkin on March 2, 1975, in Panama City. He flattened Lampkin in the 14th round, and when the ambulance attendants carted the poor guy off to the hospital, Duran shouted, "Next time, I'll kill him."

Duran won the world lightweight title on June 22, 1979, in New York when he stopped Ken Buchanan in the 13th round. He defended his crown twelve times, becoming, according to boxing observers, the greatest lightweight champion in history. "He was one of the greatest boxers I've ever seen," said Teddy Atlas, who trained former heavyweight champion Michael Moorer. "And it was because of his reflexes. He had the reflexes of a cat—so quick, with split-second timing that made it difficult to hit him." But his appetite for both food and fun proved bigger than his talent, and "Manos de Piedra" became "Belly of Jelly," eating and partying his way out of the lightweight division.

When Duran challenged Sugar Ray Leonard for the welterweight title in Montreal, he turned back to the tough-talking days of his youth. He taunted Leonard, and then he turned to Juanita, the wife of the welterweight champion, making crude, ugly comments in public—flirtatious remarks that made Leonard, usually calm and composed, seethe with anger. They fought on June 20, 1980, but Duran won the match long before fight night—at the weigh-in and press conferences where he provoked Leonard and his wife. He psyched out the man who usually did the psyching out, forcing him to fight an artless fight. Leonard, abandoning the wondrous legs that had carried him to a record of 25-0, stood toe-to-toe with the legendary "Manos de Piedra," and he paid for his foolishness. Duran pounded out a unanimous decision over the welterweight champion. "Duran did a number on Ray," said Angelo Dundee, who trained Leonard. "He got to him."

They fought again, but the good life had done what Leonard could not—it conquered Duran, and he was in no condition, mentally or physically, to defend the title he had won in such a brutal and convincing manner. Leonard, returning to the foot movement that had made him the Muhammad Ali of the welterweight division, toyed with Duran and turned the ring into a dance studio. In the 8th round Duran, confused and frustrated, uttered two of the most infamous words in boxing hisory: "No mas"—"No more"—and walked back to his corner, taking a shot in the ribs as he turned away from Leonard. Duran claimed that he was suffering an upset stomach from a steak dinner earlier that day, that it was his belly, not his opponent, who defeated him that night. Critics scoffed. They offered a different theory—that Duran, a proud fighter, could not deal with a fighter who thrived on dainty tactics such as footwork. Footwork. My God, Duran expected a street fight, not a tango, and yet here was Leonard engaged in an activity that required a chaperone, not a referee. No, Duran could not tolerate such strategy, observers said, and so he quit.

ABOVE: Roberto Duran is considered by many experts to be the greatest lightweight champion in boxing history. Among many other distinctions, he managed over the course of his career to score a knockout in every round from 1 to 15.

The fistic odd couple met a third time, on February 24, 1989, in Las Vegas, and Duran promised both a victory and an explanation—an explanation for his surrender nine years before. The boxing world got neither. Leonard scored a unanimous decision over Duran, although it was the Panamanian who looked like the winner. Duran was fresh and unmarked, while Leonard was bruised and bloodied, with a face that only Lon Chaney could love—the result of the dirty fighting that Duran had raised to an art. So much for the victory Duran promised—and so much for the explanation. Duran, apparently bitter over his defeat, told the sporting world to forget his vow. There would be no revelations, no excavations into the past, to explain an act that remains shrouded in mystery.

LEFT: Sugar Ray Leonard lands a right to the jaw of Roberto Duran during their historic Montreal fight, on June 20, 1980. Duran won a unanimous 15-round decision and the welterweight title in what had to be a devastating loss for Leonard, who for years had been the darling of the boxing community and whose incredibly successful career had been launched at the very same arena during the 1976 Olympics.

## Sugar Ray Leonard

One of the saddest spectacles in boxing history took place on March 1, 1997, in Atlantic City, New Jersey. One of the players was ex-champion Sugar Ray Leonard, then 40 years old, the greatest fighter of his era. But his era was twenty years earlier, and it showed.

The other player was Hector "Macho" Camacho, then 34, who stopped Leonard in the 5th round, landing about ten unanswered punches to the head before the referee finally stopped the bout. Leonard, who had returned after a six-year retirement, did not look like the fleet-footed, chiseled athlete he had been in his prime. He looked old, weak, and fragile.

ABOVE: Sugar Ray Charles Leonard (named after the R&B giant) battles welterweight champion Wilfred Benitez on November 30, 1979, for the title. In the closing seconds of the final round, Leonard won by knockout. In an era when television was becoming ever more popular, Leonard was the perfect candidate to bring his division popularity: he was good-looking, extremely charismatic, and had all the right moves, from his quick footwork to his patented flurries of punches. OPPOSITE: In the September 16, 1981, fight billed as "the Showdown," Sugar Ray Leonard set out to dispel the idea that his victory against Roberto Duran had somehow been a gift by taking on the supposedly invincible Thomas Hearns, "the Motor City Cobra." It was an exciting, back-and-forth affair; in the 14th round, at a point where Hearns held the upper hand on all three judges' score cards, Leonard dug deep and brought out everything he had, destroying Hearns. With the victory, Leonard unified the welterweight crown.

Sometimes great fighters are like unwelcome guests; they do not know when to leave. Ray Charles Leonard was no different. He had come back from retirement before, on February 9, 1991, when he faced Terry Norris, a young fighter eager to make his reputation against an aging legend. Leonard fell to the two most brutal opponents a fighter can face: time and the left hook. Norris battered Leonard, who had returned after a two-year exile from the ring. Before the start of the 12th and final round, Mike Trainer, the lawyer who represented the ex-champion, told him, "Try to stay on

your feet, and then we'll get out of Dodge." Leonard did stay on his feet, proving that his heart, it not his talent, was as impressive as ever. But it was time to leave, and he knew it. He grabbed the ring microphone in Madison Square Garden after the bout, addressing the crowd that had come to see a fight and had stayed to see a retirement bash.

"This is my last fight," Leonard said simply. "It took this kind of a fight to prove to me it's time for me to venture away from boxing. If there was anyone I'd like to turn this over to, it's Terry Norris. I had to find out for myself. I've always been a risk-taker." It was a bittersweet victory for Norris. "It's a sad victory," he said. "I beat my idol, and I beat him badly. I didn't want it to be that way. He's still my idol." Leonard got out of Dodge that night, but it did not last; he came

OPPOSITE: Sugar Ray Leonard and Marvelous Marvin Hagler meet in the center of the ring during their April 6, 1987, middleweight title bout, a match Leonard won by a split decision. It was a tremendous comeback victory for the 31-year-old Leonard, who had been retired for five years before the fight. ABOVE: Referee Richard Steele restrains a surging Sugar Ray Leonard during during the 9th round of a fight against Donny Lalonde, November 7, 1988. Leonard won the fight by TKO in the same round.

back, against Camacho. "The Macho Man" beat him—
and beat him easily. Why do great fighters subject
themselves to such indignities?

Leonard would not learn; great fighters seldom do.
After all, he had been an awesome fighter in his prime.
And hadn't other, even older fighters defied the rav-
ages of time and triumphed? Unfortunately Leonard
had to find out the hard way that old fighters sometimes really do just fade away.

But if those final two fights—against Norris and
Camacho—left sad, bitter memories, it is only because
they stand out in a career that was as glorious as it
was electrifying. Leonard was a great fighter, his
achievements amplified because he filled the void that
Muhammad Ali created when he retired in 1981. He
was the Ali of the lighter weight divisions, a showman
who wore short pants and gloves instead of a top hat
and tails. Like Sugar Ray Robinson before him, he
could dazzle you or flatten you; he was that versatile.
And he proved it in fight after fight, defeating the
greatest boxers of his generation—Roberto Duran,
Thomas Hearns, Wilfred Benitez, and "Marvelous"
Marvin Hagler.

In retrospect, it is easy to see why Leonard
thought he could beat Norris and Camacho. After all,
he had come back before, returning from a five-year
absence to defeat one of the greatest fighters of the
1980s—Hagler. Leonard scored a split decision over
Hagler on April 6, 1987, in Las Vegas, forcing the middleweight champion into a retirement that he was wise
enough to maintain. If only Leonard had been so wise.

## Thomas Hearns

It was June 12, 1989, in Las Vegas, and the sportswriters crafted their stories for the obituary sections of
their newspapers. Why? Because Thomas Hearns, as a
fighter, was dead—or so the sportswriters thought. The
only difference between Hearns and a can of tomatoes,
the critics said, was in the nutritional value. Or was it?
Hearns did not believe it, and he set out to disprove

RIGHT: Thomas Hearns, "the Motor City Cobra," staged a comeback in the late 1980s that
included this June 12, 1989, rematch against Sugar Ray Leonard, who had beaten him in dramatic
fashion in the 14th round of their September 16, 1981, match-up. The 1989 fight was scored a draw
by the judges, though many observers felt Hearns had fought the better bout.

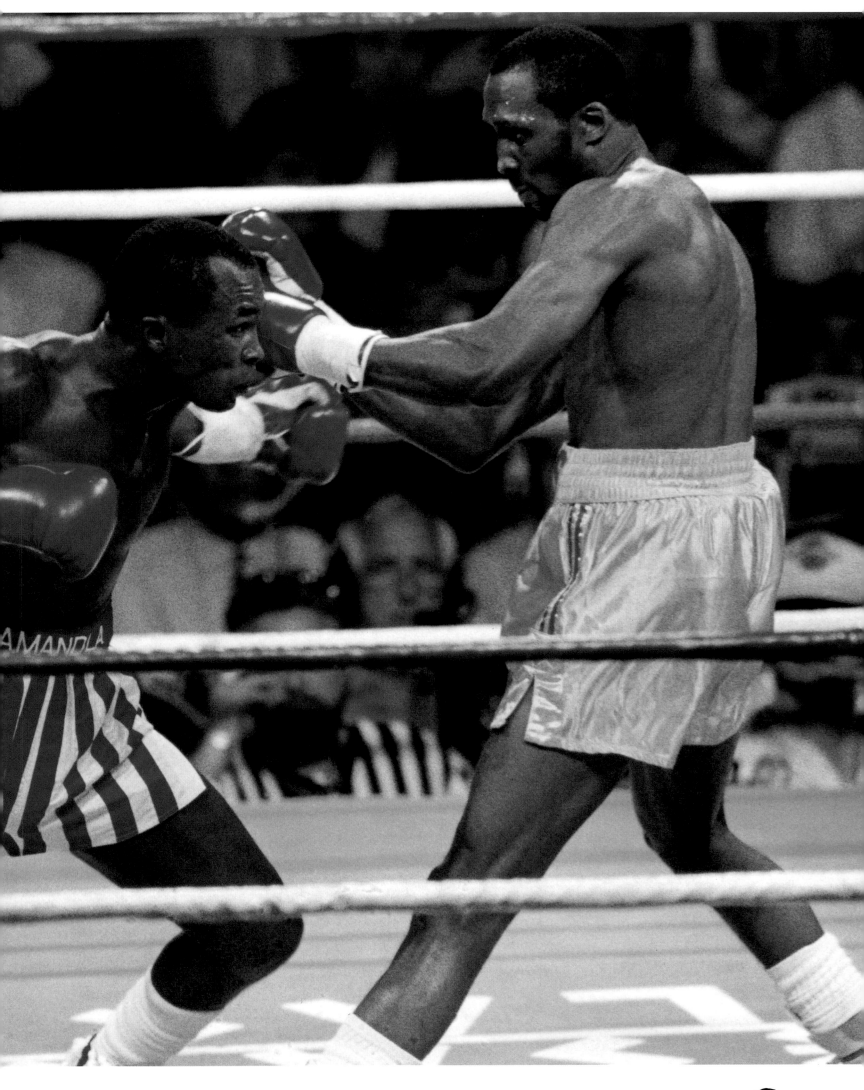

what his recent past seemed to confirm. After all, here was a man who had been clubbed by "Marvelous" Marvin Hagler and Iran Barkley, a knockout victim each time. And now he was facing Sugar Ray Leonard, who had already beaten him on September 16, 1981—a 14th-round knockout in one of the greatest fights of all time.

To Hearns, the rematch was not a fight; it was a revival meeting. He wanted to find out if he could redeem himself. He wanted to find out if he could achieve grace in a 20-foot (6m) ring, where one punch can mean the difference between doom and salvation. He wanted to find out, more than anything, if he could whup Sugar Ray Leonard. Hearns did just that, dropping him twice in a tense and exciting match, but he would not get the decision. The judges scored the fight a draw, a travesty for the man who wanted to prove so much. He accepted the decision gracefully. "I leave it up to the judges," he said. "I'm proud of the draw. I have to be thankful for what I received."

For a fighter who seemed washed up before the Leonard fight, Hearns proved remarkably durable after the bout, going on to defeat Virgil Hill for the light heavyweight title on June 3, 1991, in Las Vegas. Hearns was a tremendous puncher early in his career; his tall, thin frame belied his power. But punching power is not about bulk or muscles; it is about speed and balance, timing and coordination, and Hearns boasted all of these qualities, hammering opponents on the inside or strafing them from the outside.

Hearns retained that power, but he also became a smart fighter in the twilight of his career, his kamikaze style tempered by craft and guile. Witness his bout against the hard-punching James Kinchen on November 4, 1988, in Las Vegas. Kinchen staggered Hearns in the middle rounds, and Hearns grabbed his opponent as if he were a dance partner, holding him so tight that the referee could barely pry the two men apart. "I held onto him like he was my woman," Hearns said. Like Leonard, Hearns fought the greatest fighters of his era— Leonard, Hagler, Roberto Duran, Pepino Cuevas. He did not always win, but when he lost, he lost spectacularly, throwing punches until his chin betrayed him. That will be his ultimate legacy to boxing—the tension

RIGHT: An extremely determined Hearns outjabs Virgil Hill to reclaim the light heavyweight title on June 3, 1991.

and excitement he brought to the sport. He was not the showman that Ali and Leonard were, but he was every bit as entertaining, the thrills coming from the heart and fury he displayed in the ring.

## "Marvelous" Marvin Hagler

The first name was not a name at all. It was an adjective, but it applied—"Marvelous" Marvin Hagler. Then again, maybe the name should have been "Menacing" Marvin Hagler, because he intimidated opponents long before they stepped into the ring. Maybe it was the scowl, the shaved head, or the pet names he gave his fists, "Knock" and "Out." Or maybe it was his motto, a paean to brutality, if not grammar—"Destruct and destroy."

It must have been all of those things, because it was certainly not his ring presence. Hagler was not a monster in the ring, not in the sense that Roberto Duran or Thomas "the Hit Man" Hearns was. He was a cautious, scientific boxer, a southpaw who could fight as a right-hander, switching stances so smoothly and fluidly, sometimes in the middle of a combination, that opponents were stunned, first by his movement, then by his punches.

ABOVE: Marvelous Marvin Hagler appears focused in the moments before his September 27, 1980, fight against Alan Minter. After years of frustration, typified by the Antuofermo fight in 1979 that by most accounts had been won by Hagler, "Marvelous" slugged his way to the middleweight championship with a decisive 3rd-round knockout of Minter. OPPOSITE: Marvelous Marvin Hagler and Vito Antuofermo rough each other up on the inside on November 30, 1979, during a title bout that ended in a draw. Since his professional debut in 1973, Hagler created quite a reputation for himself in the middleweight division, proving he could win from both sides and with amazing changes in rhythm. But of course, he wanted more. His first attempt to win the title was here against Antuofermo and many outraged observers thought that Hagler had been robbed of a victory by the decision.

"Destruct and destroy?" Perhaps, but it seemed more like "Dazzle and destroy." "He's the monster man," trainer Angelo Dundee said, perpetuating an image that seemed inaccurate.

Or was it inaccurate? Hagler could be a monster, but he pressed the attack only if he was pressed in return. And he was pressed on April 15, 1985, in Las Vegas, when he knocked out Hearns in one of the most sensational fights in boxing history. "It was 3 minutes of mayhem, of controlled, educated violence sustained at an almost unendurable level of intensity," wrote Harry Mullan, editor of the British magazine *Boxing News*. "They smashed terrifying hooks at each other, full-blooded blows which were designed to intimidate and destroy."

Like many great fighters before him, Hagler found more obstacles outside the ring than inside. Rather than duck his punches, champions ducked him, refusing to give him a shot at their titles. He lost two matches in Philadelphia, home to some of the greatest middleweights in the world—to Bobby "Boogaloo" Watts and Willie "the Worm" Monroe—but he returned to prove himself in the same town, beating Eugene Hart, Bennie Briscoe, and, in a rematch, Monroe. And it was then that the ducking started. Hagler became bitter and frustrated, a contender for life—or so he thought. Legislators championed his cause, trying to lobby on his behalf. When he finally got his shot against middleweight champion Vito Antuofermo on November 30, 1979, in Las Vegas, the judges scored the fight a draw—an injustice that enraged an already bitter man. The bitterness did not last long. He got another shot, this one against Alan Minter on

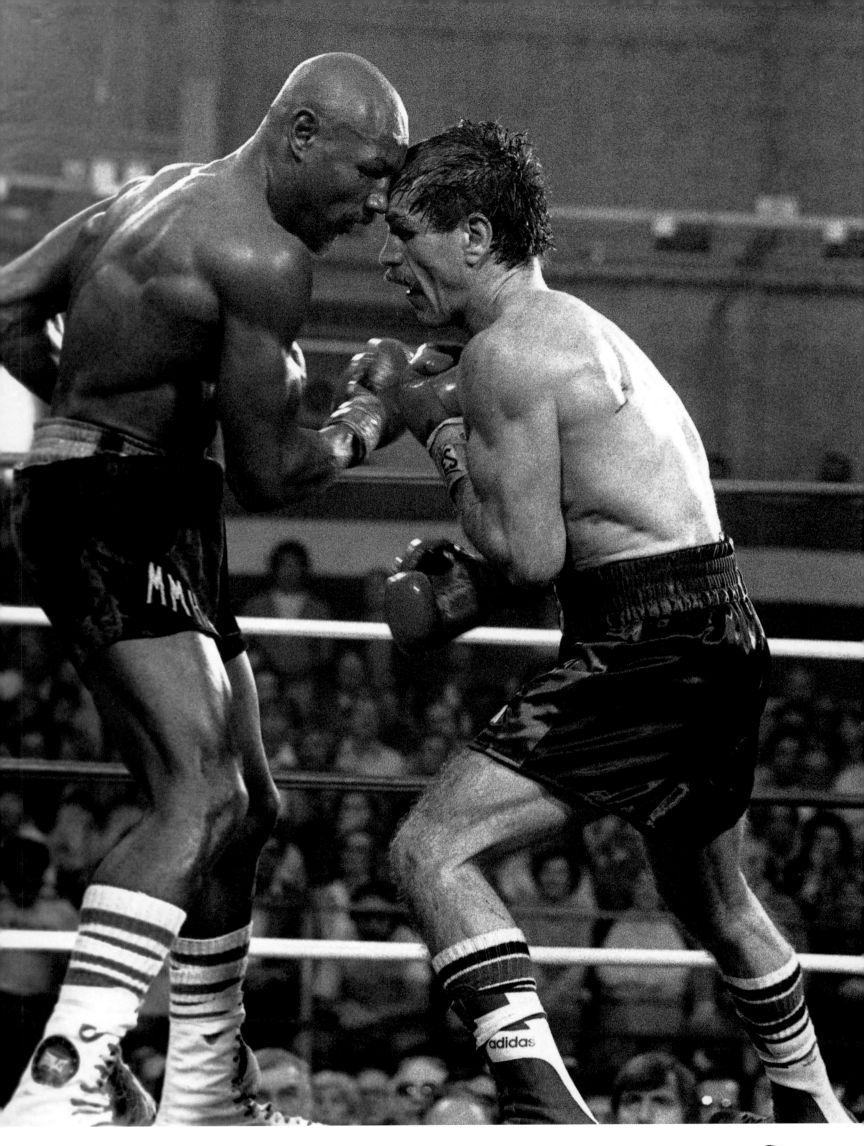

September 27, 1980, in London, and he exploited the opportunity by removing the judges from consideration. He knocked out Alan Minter in the 3rd round, sparking a riot that forced the new champion to hide under the ring. "The violence doesn't really bother me," Hagler said afterward, shrugging his shoulders.

Hagler held onto his title for seven years, which included thirteen successful defenses, an astounding streak that ended when Sugar Ray Leonard upset him on April 6, 1987. It was a controversial decision, and Hagler responded with the anger that had fueled him

ABOVE: Marvelous Marvin Hagler hammers Thomas Hearns to the floor in their classic middleweight bout, April 15, 1985. RIGHT: Marvin Hagler rocks challenger John Mugabi with a thunderous left during the 2nd round of this title defense on March 10, 1986, in Las Vegas.

earlier in his career, when he could not get the title shot he deserved. He was so bitter that he retired and moved to Italy, where he became a star of action movies—a real-life warrior turned into a celluloid hero, his motto still "Destruct and destroy."

## George Foreman

If Muhammad Ali towered above the rest of the world, George Foreman stood with the common man, pleasant and humble and unassuming. But he was not a common man. He was the oldest heavyweight champion to walk the planet. Foreman reached that status with a remarkable performance on November 5, 1994, when he knocked out Michael Moorer in the 11th round. Foreman, the fistic Everyman, was 45 years old, seven years older than Jersey Joe Walcott was when he defeated Ezzard Charles for the heavyweight title on June 5, 1952. "My promoter kept saying that I could make history," Foreman said afterward, wearing a pair of sunglasses to conceal the bruises on his face. "He said, 'History, George, history.' And I knew he was no Barnum and Bailey. I knew he was being sincere."

Foreman was bigger than boxing, and not just becaust he stood 6 feet 3 inches (191cm) and weighed 250 pounds (114kg). No, he transcended the sport because he could relate to his fans and his fans could

ABOVE: George Foreman smashes a left to the head of Joe Frazier, flooring the heavyweight champion for the sixth and final time on January 22, 1973. This devastating display of power—Frazier went to the mat three times in the 1st round and three times in the 95 seconds the referee allowed of the subsequent round—gave Foreman the championship. Interestingly, it was the first time in almost sixty years that the heavyweight title had been decided in a locale outside the United States. OPPOSITE: A reborn George Foreman stalks the ring after knocking Gerry Cooney out in the 2nd round of their January 15, 1990, heavyweight bout. Few observers realized it at the time, but the apparently over-the-hill Foreman was just four years away from making boxing history.

relate to him. He was a rarity: a man who delighted in his imperfections. When he strolled toward the ring, his stomach visible several seconds before the rest of his body, he seemed to say, "It's okay to be heavy. Feel good about yourself." And so the boxing world felt good about this benign brawler.

Before his comeback in 1987, Foreman was not sweet, caring, and pleasant. He was moody and self-absorbed, interested more in his pet lions than in the people around him. And, my, could he punch. He owned the heaviest hammers this side of a hardware store, both of them encased in 10-ounce (285g) leather gloves. One shot from either of them—left or right—and the ring would turn into a grotesque roller-coaster ride, with the man who took the punch hanging on for dear life. "I have the cannon effect," Foreman said. "On a battleship, you have these guns that go boom! The gunners know that if one shot hits, that's all it's gonna take. That's what my hands are like."

Foreman learned how to box in the Job Corps, where he acquired a skill that would win him an Olympic gold medal in 1968 and the world heavyweight title five years later. He won the championship with his 2-round demolition of Joe Frazier on January 22, 1973, in Kingston, Jamaica, perhaps the most impressive display of punching power in heavyweight history. Then he lost the crown a year later, when Muhammad Ali stopped him in the 8th

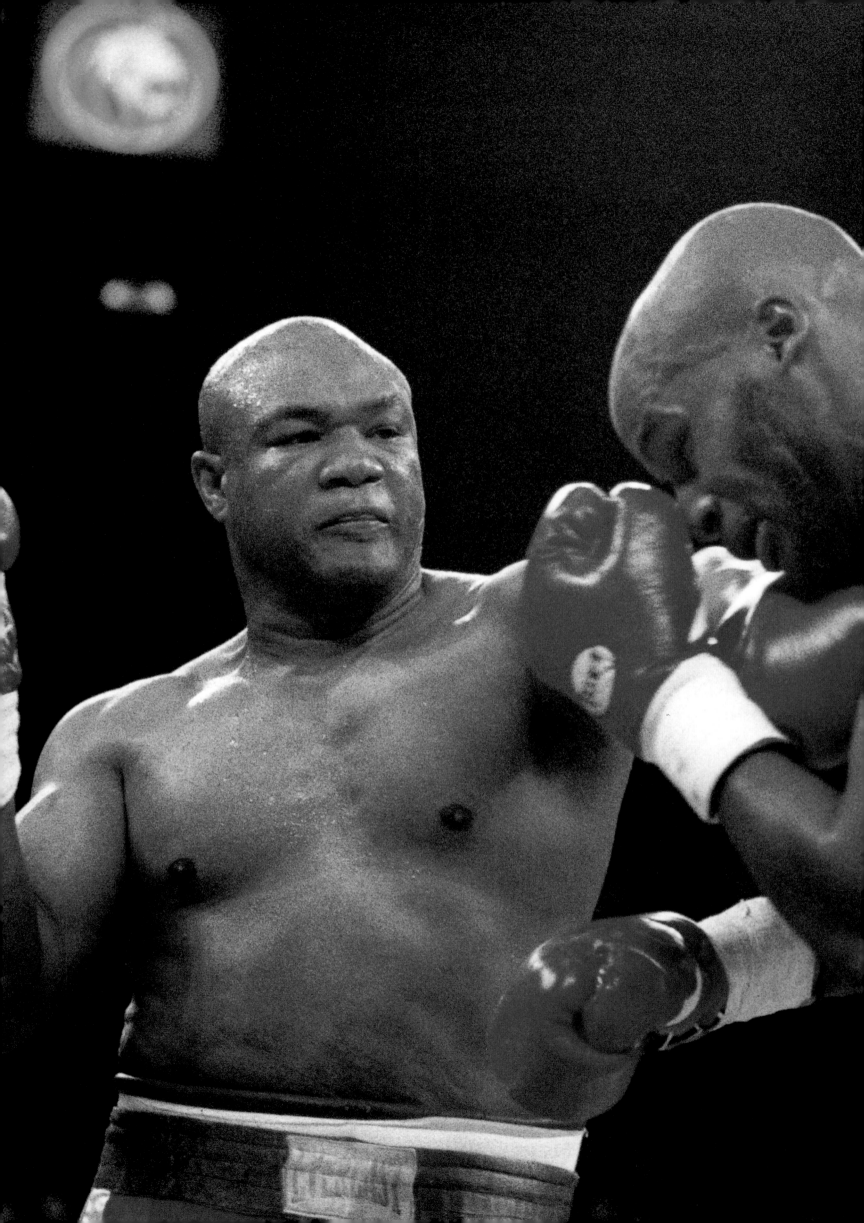

# A Closer Look

George Foreman stood in the center of the ring, almost 30 minutes into a horrible beating, his breath gone and his strength about to follow, when something amazing happened. Something miraculous. The George Foreman of 1994 became the George Foreman of 1974—a time warp that shocked the world.

One second the old man was marooned in his own body, conscious but unable to make his arms and legs respond to the messages from his brain. And the next second? Young and vibrant again, he was trying to decapitate Michael Moorer, the heavyweight champion of the world. Moorer kept his head, but he could not keep the crown that sat upon it. The old man, behind on all three cards, knocked him out in the 10th round, flattening him with one of the greatest combinations in boxing history—a left jab followed by a chopping right, both of them short and sweet and punishing. And, oh yes, amazing. Foreman became the oldest heavyweight champion in history, seven years older than the previous oldest champion, Jersey Joe Walcott. It happened on November 5, 1994, in Las Vegas, and boxing fans will remember it forever. "This is the greatest thrill of my athletic career," Foreman said.

With his victory over Moorer, he regained the title he had lost to Muhammad Ali twenty years before, during the legendary "Rumble in the Jungle" on October 30, 1974. "I've been heavyweight champion of the world before, and I know what it feels like," Foreman said. "But, when I saw Moorer on his back, all I wanted to do was let the Almighty know that I appreciate living this long."

Foreman, who had been retired for ten years, launched his comeback against Steve Zouski on March 9, 1987—a comeback that inspired laughter throughout the boxing world. The old man hit the canvas about six times—not from punches he absorbed, but from punches he threw. He would fire the overhand right, delivering the punch with the follow-through of a baseball pitcher, and fall down when he missed. It was an embarrassing episode, but he won the fight, and it taught him a lesson: he began to shorten his punches—and stay on his feet.

The fans stopped laughing on January 15, 1990, when Foreman crushed Gerry Cooney in the 2nd round. Then he fought Evander Holyfield for the undisputed title a year later, acquiring even more fans and admirers with his courageous, albeit losing, performance against a man twelve years younger. Spectators left the arena as if they had just witnessed a heartwarming musical, not a brutal heavyweight fight. "I had more fun this time than the first time," Foreman said. "I didn't take myself seriously, but every time I stood in front of a microphone, I was very conscious of what I said, because I knew the kids were listening. That's how I want to be remembered—as someone who cared about the kids."

A man who seemed to thrive on intimidation both inside and outside the ring during his first incarnation, Foreman became gentler during his ten years away from the ring, when he discovered that people were nice to him even though they had nothing to gain from their association with him.

"I was a nobody," Foreman said. "People didn't even know I was champ. They just called me the 'Big-un.' I was so spoiled when I was champ. I didn't do anything for myself. Then I retired, and I was lost. I didn't even know how to pump gas at those self-serve stations. People were always ready to help the 'Big-un.' I learned to appreciate human beings. When you've lost a human being, you've lost something special."

And that is exactly what the fans thought of Foreman—they thought he was something special. "George has been so unbelievable for this sport," the late Dan Duva once said. "Without him, there would be no humor in this business. He's done far more for this sport than anyone ever thought he would."

OPPOSITE: George Foreman lands a punishing left en route to a stunning, historic victory over Michael Moorer on November 5, 1994. The win, which gave Foreman both the WBA and the IBF heavyweight crowns, caused the boxing world to reevaluate Foreman's place in the pantheon of boxing deities. ABOVE: Becoming the oldest man to win the heavyweight title, George Foreman stares at the man he clubbed into submission, Michael Moorer.

round in Kinshasa, Zaire—an upset as shocking as the one Foreman had administered against Frazier. "If I had been smart, Ali would never have beaten me," Foreman said. "But Ali was tricking me, making me punch myself out, and I didn't even realize it." Then 29, Foreman announced his retirement after losing a decision to Jimmy Young, a wily but light-hitting boxer, on March 17, 1977, in San Juan, Puerto Rico. It was not the loss that caused Foreman to walk away from boxing. It was what happened after the loss.

"I was back in the dressing room after the fight, and I had this gigantic experience," Foreman said. "For a split second, just a split second, I was dead. I told everyone I was dying. They thought I was going crazy. I was in a deep, dark nothing place, and there was a horrible smell to go along with the nothingness.

"Then a giant hand reached out and saved me. And when I had this vision, I collapsed. I told my doctor, 'Take your hat off, because the thorns on it are making your head bleed.' I started reciting verses from the Bible that I didn't even know."

The doctor called it heat prostration, but Foreman called it a revelation. The ex-champion became a Protestant minister a year later, waging battles that were strictly of the spiritual variety. He built a church in north Houston, the Church of the Lord Jesus Christ, and he began to discard the "material things" he had acquired with his ring earnings, including his seven cars. "I started realizing there was more to this world than George Foreman," he said. Foreman was content to remain a full-time preacher until 1986, when he refused, for what he thought were sound reasons, to help a member of his flock. "One kid was getting into trouble, so his mother came to me for help," Foreman said. "She asked me if I could show her son how to box. She thought boxing would keep him out of trouble, the same way it did for me. I said, 'Now how can I teach a kid how to fight when I'm a preacher?' It wouldn't look right. The kid ended up going to prison." So Foreman experienced another revelation, this one just as vivid, if not as dramatic, as the one in San Juan. "I had no right to refuse to help the kid just because I was afraid of what people would think," Foreman said. "So I thought I could help the church by boxing and raising money. I put on my short pants again. They were tight." Thus began his quest, which ended when he beat Moorer.

Foreman enjoyed his dual life, rhapsodizing in the church one minute, terrorizing in the ring the next. If there was any contradiction between saving souls and putting them to sleep, he did not see it. The fighting preacher was having too much fun doing both. And the boxing world was glad he did.

## Larry Holmes

After one of his comeback fights in 1991, Larry Holmes jumped into the air, staying aloft for so long that he looked like a statue mounted on a pedestal of air. Then, quoting another aging entertainer, James Brown, the former heavyweight champion shouted, "I feeeeeeel good!" Feel good? Larry Holmes? The man who once told the world to kiss him on a part of his anatomy concealed by his silk trunks? Yes, that Larry Holmes. Like George Foreman, another former champion who returned to the ring, Holmes was a different man during his comeback—wiser, if not kinder and gentler. "There was real animosity between Larry and me in the old days," said Bob Arum, who promoted Holmes during his comeback. "He was rude, impolite, and he would shout at me in public. I refused to talk to him for years. But he changed. He enjoyed himself more the second time around. He and George became much calmer. They've proved what you can accomplish by being a gentleman."

If Holmes was bitter the first time around, there was good reason for it. He followed the toughest act in sports history: Muhammad Ali. Holmes was a great fighter, but great was not good enough, not for the man who chased Ali. Think of it. Who were the guys that followed Elvis into Sun Studio in Memphis, Tennessee? Jerry Lee Lewis, Carl Perkins, Johnny Cash? They were titanic talents, all of them, but they were not Elvis. And Holmes was not Ali. He tried to be Ali, tried to imitate his magnificent style, according to the critics, and who could blame him? After all, the kid sparred with "the Greatest" in the mid-1970s, and he was so good that Ali called him the future heavy-

OPPOSITE: In one of the greatest heavyweight title fights ever waged—even though the title had been split by now among various organizations and was something of a travesty—Larry Holmes strafes Ken Norton with a right on June 9, 1978. The fight went the distance and was a classic back-and-forth contest, with the two giants trading ground-shaking power punches throughout. In the 15th round, Holmes dug a little deeper and in a closing flurry secured the split decision—by 1 point. Unheralded until then, Holmes had finally won some notoriety—if not exactly respect.

weight champion of the world. The kid, trying to punch his way out of the projects in Easton, Pennsylvania, was mesmerized. "He was the heavyweight champion of the world, and I was a kid," Holmes said. "Shoot, man, you couldn't tell me nothing. I was on cloud nine."

For Holmes, his greatest triumph would prove his greatest downfall. He defeated Ken Norton on June 9, 1978, in Las Vegas, scoring a split decision to win the heavyweight title in one of the greatest bouts in boxing history—a tough, grueling match, with both fighters so tired that they ended up in a sweaty embrace, their bodies draped across each other like shabby overcoats. "I wanted to take him out," Holmes said. "I hurt him a few times, and he hurt me, but because of his determination and my determination, we both finished."

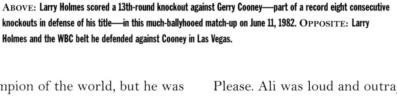

ABOVE: Larry Holmes scored a 13th-round knockout against Gerry Cooney—part of a record eight consecutive knockouts in defense of his title—in this much-ballyhooed match-up on June 11, 1982. OPPOSITE: Larry Holmes and the WBC belt he defended against Cooney in Las Vegas.

The kid became what Ali had predicted, the heavyweight champion of the world, but he was not a champion so much as a successor to the champion, a successor to the man. The critics called him a carbon copy of Ali, and he bristled. Holmes fell from cloud nine, nose-diving through the mists of the ozone, the rarified heights becoming the agonizing lows. And he landed on his butt.

Holmes was arrogant, and he admitted it freely. "I always thought I could get along with people by telling 'em where it's at from the beginning," he said. It was a noble stance, perhaps, but a misguided one. Holmes, hounded by the ghost of Ali, became moody and defensive, detecting slights where none were intended. For Holmes, the idol had become the tormentor, and Holmes tried to squash the anguish in the only forum where he felt comfortable: the ring. He met Ali

on October 2, 1980, in Las Vegas—the sparring partner versus the professor—but Holmes did not get the satisfaction he wanted. He beat the old man, all right, beat him badly, with Ali cowering on the ropes like a helpless child, unable to stop the punishment he would have avoided in his prime. But America felt bad about the spectacle, and Holmes felt worse, so when the referee stopped the bout in the 11th round, the anguish continued, and Larry Holmes went on being Larry Holmes, the successor to Muhammad Ali.

When Holmes lost to Michael Spinks on September 21, 1985, becoming the first heavyweight champion to lose his title to a light heavyweight champion, he blamed the defeat on politics. When he lost the rematch seven months later, he went ballistic, telling a national television audience that the cable network HBO could kiss him "where the sun didn't shine." A carbon copy of Ali? Please. Ali was loud and outrageous, but he had an undeniable grace and dignity that his successor seemed to lack.

After retiring in 1986, Holmes returned to challenge Mike Tyson, then the heavyweight champion of the world, on January 22, 1988, in Atlantic City. Tyson stopped the ex-champion in the 4th round, with Holmes falling flat on his back, his legs shooting up awkwardly as he crashed to the canvas. The ex-champ started to gag, and the referee, afraid the fallen fighter was choking on his mouthpiece, tried to yank it out. "I'm going to laugh all the way to the Lafayette Savings and Loan," Holmes said before returning to his home in Easton.

If Holmes had ended his career there, the world would still know him as the carbon copy of Ali—loud

and arrogant and profane. But he came back, and he came back a different man, proud to be Larry Holmes—not a carbon copy, but an original. Holmes began to enjoy himself—perhaps the biggest shock of his career. When he upset Ray Mercer on February 7, 1992, in Atlantic City, the crowd cheered him in the early rounds, chanting, "Larry, Larry, Larry." The ex-champion fed off the energy, but instead of getting pumped up, he became more relaxed; at one point, trapped in the corner, Holmes looked into a television camera, said, "Watch this," and popped Mercer with a straight right to the forehead. It was as close as a fight gets to a lounge act. And the fans loved it. "To tell you the truth, I thought the Mercer fight was going to be the end of Larry," Arum said. "Mercer hits hard and has a great chin. But Larry proved us all wrong."

During his second comeback, Holmes challenged two heavyweight champions, Evander Holyfield and Oliver McCall, losing both fights by decision. But he won something more important during his return to the ring—the respect of the fans who had scorned him for years. And he savored it. "People used to say I was just a carbon copy of Ali," he said. "Now I don't care what they say."

## Michael Spinks

Michael Spinks was Gumby in short pants, bending, twisting, and throwing punches—so many punches from so many angles that he looked like a picnicker shooing away a squadron of flies. "If I walked into a gym, and I saw Spinks training for the first time, yes, I would be tempted to change his style," said Eddie Futch, who trained the former light heavyweight and heavyweight champion. But Futch was wise and didn't tamper with an ugly style that produced beautiful results.

ABOVE: On September 21, 1985, Michael Spinks avenged his brother Leon's June 2, 1981, loss to Larry Holmes. With the dramatic upset, Michael and Leon became the only brothers to have been world heavyweight champions. Here, Spinks is congratulated by promoter Butch Lewis (right).

From 1981 to 1985, Spinks dominated the light heavyweight division, dazzling opponents with his movement, then clubbing them with the overhand right that he called "the Spinks Jinx." He won the title on July 18, 1981, in Las Vegas, scoring a unanimous decision over Mustafa Muhammad. The champ remained in the division for four more years, defending his title ten times, before the irony of his situation

ing the boxing world when he stepped on the scale—he weighed 200 pounds (91kg), 21 pounds (10kg) less than Holmes. Okay, the critics said, he looked like a heavyweight, with the thick upper body of his new mates in the division, but could he fight like a heavyweight? The answer was yes. Spinks upset Holmes on September 21, 1985, in Las Vegas, to become the first reigning light heavyweight champion to win the

ABOVE: Normally a light heavyweight, Michael Spinks had bulked up to challenge Larry Holmes for the heavyweight title. In a stunning upset victory, Spinks beat his opponent to win the heavyweight crown on September 21, 1985. Spinks won a unanimous decision over Holmes, who would lose to Spinks again in a 1986 rematch.

hit him like a right cross to the temple. Here he was, the undisputed master of his division, but his success was straitjacketing him, leaving him with no more opponents, no more bouts to test his ability, to raise the bar. So he fled.

If Spinks escaped, his destination did not exactly look like a sanctuary. He climbed to the heavyweight division, a weight class ruled by the most dominant champion of the era: Larry Holmes. It was a downright crazy idea. Spinks hired fitness guru Mackie Shilstone to give him a new body—the body of a heavyweight. He lifted weights and ran wind sprints, abandoning the long-distance road work that boxers had favored since the turn of the century. The hard work paid off; Spinks became a heavyweight, shock-

heavyweight title. Then he won the rematch seven months later, when he survived an early battering to score a hotly disputed split decision over the ex-champion.

With his rival now retired, Spinks fought a man who threatened to become as dominant as Holmes: Mike Tyson. They called it "the Fight of the Century," but it is hard for a fight to be considered one for the ages when it lasts only 91 seconds. Tyson destroyed Spinks on June 27, 1988, in Atlantic City by decking him with a right uppercut to the jaw. The ex–light heavyweight, who had never been floored, looked like a light heavyweight again, weak and frail, his head crashing to the canvas, his eyes receding into his skull. It was a sad end to a glorious ride.

The former two-time champion retired a few months later, his latest defeat failing to overshadow what had been a brilliant career. He left the ring with a record of 31-1 with 21 knockouts—not bad for a kid who seemed like a reluctant warrior. Spinks entered boxing for the same reason that his older brother Leon did—to learn how to defend himself. He was 13 when he walked into a gym for the first time, and he cried during his first few sparring sessions. Leon called him a sissy, and Michael, on the verge of abandoning the sport he had just picked up, decided to persevere. "Michael got so good that he would give Leon a pretty hard time in the gym," said Claudell Atkins, a childhood friend. "Their sparring sessions weren't wars or anything. They weren't out to kill each other. But if Leon ever dropped his hands too low— whomp—Michael would nail him."

Both Michael and Leon went on to win the heavyweight title, becoming the only brothers to share that status in boxing history, although Michael was the superior fighter, the man whose ring record marked him as an immortal.

ABOVE: Reigning heavyweight champion Mike Tyson looks on as former champion Larry Holmes topples into the ropes on January 22, 1988. The fight was an ill-advised comeback attempt by Holmes against an opponent who at the time was absolutely lethal in the ring in fight after fight. OPPOSITE: Mike Tyson and Donovan "Razor" Ruddock first met on March 18, 1991; at the time, Tyson was still on the comeback trail following his stunning loss to Buster Douglas. Tyson won the Ruddock fight by TKO, but many observers felt the refs had stopped the fight prematurely and that Tyson had gotten away with an easy win. The two men met again, on June 28 that year, and Tyson proved that the abbreviated first encounter had been a lucky one for Ruddock. In the second fight, shown here, Tyson sent Ruddock to the mat twice and broke the larger man's jaw en route to winning a 12-round decision. Here, "Iron" Mike smashes "Razor" Ruddock in the face with a piledriver left during the second fight (Tyson's last before going to prison on a rape conviction), dislodging Ruddock's mouth guard in the process.

## Mike Tyson

It was 1985, and the kid was sparring at a gym in Catskill, New York, getting ready to launch an attack that could turn a forest into a field of pencil shavings. "I want to be the greatest heavyweight who ever lived," he said. "That's my goal."

The kid was Mike Tyson, and he spoke with the sweet passion of youth, his lisp as disarming as his left hook. This was "Kid Dynamite," the young man whom *Ring Magazine* called "the savior of boxing." The fans loved him, but the love affair would not last. In the end,

the savior of boxing could not save himself, much less the fight game. Was it a losing battle? Perhaps, but he kept trying, his reclamation project suddenly downsized in scope from the boxing world to one individual in the boxing world—himself. It will be his biggest challenge.

From 1986 to 1990, Tyson was the terror of the heavyweight division—a reign that started when he defeated Trevor Berbick to become the youngest heavyweight champion in history. The champion went 10-0 with 8 knockouts during that span, including victories over Larry Holmes and Tony Tucker, and he did it with a style that was as efficient as it was brutal, combining superb defense with explosive offense. He taunted opponents before and after fights, once saying that Tyrell Biggs moaned like a woman when he received a shot to the ribs. "Mike has a lot of ability, but I think he's only reached about 30 percent of his potential," Kevin Rooney, his ex-trainer, said during that period. "When he gets older, he's going to be scary. I wouldn't want to say he can become the greatest. I mean when you say the greatest, what's next? Being God? But I will say this: he can become a great, great champion, one of the best that ever lived."

Then he met a journeyman on February 11, 1990, in Tokyo, and the journeyman earned one of the biggest—and quickest—promotions in the history of the working class, going from pug to heavyweight champion in one startling night. James "Buster" Douglas knocked out Tyson in the 10th round with a combination that shocked the world.

Tyson came back, trying to reclaim his position as the "baddest" man on the planet. He won four fights, but he was no longer the baddest man in the world: he had to change his motto or find a new planet, because

the best heavyweight in the world was Evander Holyfield. Holyfield had dethroned Douglas with a 3rd-round knockout on October 25, 1990, in Las Vegas. If Tyson wanted to regain his status, he had to beat Holyfield, a quiet man with none of the menace—or disturbing charisma—of the erstwhile "Kid Dynamite."

The fight was scheduled for the fall of 1991, but it was postponed for five years. Tyson was convicted of raping a teenage beauty contestant at a posh hotel in Indianapolis, Indiana, on July 19, 1991, a conviction that sent him to prison for three years. He was the biggest draw in boxing—and its most tragic figure—with his once glorious career lost in the rubble of his own excesses, his own paranoia. "The sport will continue with or without Mike Tyson," said Gil Clancy, the color commentator for CBS. "I go back to the time Rocky Marciano retired. They said boxing was going to die, and it didn't. When Muhammad Ali retired, they said boxing was going to die, and it didn't. When Sugar Ray Leonard retired, they said boxing was going to die, and it didn't. Boxing will survive."

Released from prison in the spring of 1995, Tyson won four comeback fights, including a 1st-round knockout of Bruce Seldon to capture the world heavyweight title. He looked like his old self again, but his old rival was still out there: Holyfield, who had lost, regained, and lost the title since defeating Douglas six years before. Tyson met Holyfield on November 9, 1996, in Las Vegas in one of the most anticipated bouts in the history of the division. Holyfield crushed Tyson, landing about fifteen unanswered punches—each one more solid than the last—before the referee finally stopped the bout 37 seconds into the 11th round. Holyfield joined Ali as the only three-time heavyweight champion in boxing history. "I fought each round competitively," Holyfield said. "I fought the fight a round at a time."

When they met again eight months later, Tyson turned the ring into a buffet, biting the champion on both ears before the referee stopped the fight in the 3rd round. It was one of the most bizarre spectacles in ring history, and it shocked the world. The question is, why did he do it? Tyson, after all, was perfect for his sport, a thug whose fists were like blackjacks or tire irons—weapons that he brandished with a savage pride. But "Iron Mike" went too far this time. It is not easy to go too far in this sport, but Tyson did, and the Nevada Athletic Commission revoked his license for the biting incident. "Please don't torture me any longer," he told the commission a year later. "I made a mistake. Other fighters have made more. I'm just a human being trying to live my life."

The commission reinstated his license in 1998, but Tyson received a stern warning from the chairman. "I want to warn you, from my view, this will be your last chance," Elias Ghanem said. "You will either conduct yourself in accordance with our rules and regulations, or you will probably never fight again in Nevada." It was the last chance for a man whose first chance—eighteen years earlier—had begun what had promised to be such a heartwarming story.

The tale of "Kid Dynamite" began in Brooklyn, New York, where Tyson turned the world into his ring by fighting on the streets, robbing people, and finally landing in a juvenile detention facility at the Tryon School in Johnstown, New York. He wandered into a gym one day—the gym above the police station in Catskill, New York—and Cus D'Amato, who managed former heavyweight champion Floyd Patterson, spotted him. He dubbed him the future heavyweight champion of the world. Tyson was thirteen years old. D'Amato, who became his surrogate parent in 1979, died on November 4, 1985. "I think [Tyson] was struggling with who he wanted to be," said Teddy Atlas, a trainer who was himself a protégé of D'Amato. "And you know what? We all do. But all of us don't grow up to be heavyweight champion of the world, and all of us don't have to cope with that kind of attention. He created this image of a villain, and it got stronger and stronger. And he had to keep going through with the act."

Now the commission—and the world—are wondering when the curtain will finally fall on that performance.

## James "Buster" Douglas

It was a short reign—just long enough for James "Buster" Douglas to fatten both his bank account and his belly.

Yes, Douglas would live the good life, damaging his career in his pursuit of pleasure. But back in 1990, none of that seemed to matter, because for a few glori-

# A Closer Look

When James "Buster" Douglas clubbed Mike Tyson on February 10, 1990, the world tried to embrace him as a folk hero. There was only one problem—how do you get your arms around a guy who goes from heavyweight champion to overweight champion quicker than you can say "Pass the potatoes"? Douglas ate his way out of the title, losing the crown in his first defense, to Evander Holyfield, less than a year later. "He went down like a dog," Don King, who had promoted Tyson, crowed lustily after the fight. "And then he howled at the moon." Subdued by sloth and arrogance, Douglas retired to do what he did best: eat. He earned—stole?—$21 million for the fight, and he invested most of it in his appetite, stuffing his face as if he were stoking a fire in his belly. Douglas began to eat his life away, just as he had once eaten his title away, and it was tragic. He ballooned to 400 pounds (182kg), and he became almost unrecognizable, his eyes disappearing into his face. "It didn't matter what I ate," Douglas said. "As long as it was food, just food. I would eat anything."

It was self-destructive, but Douglas kept on eating, his appetite overcoming his common sense. Then, in the summer of

ABOVE: Buster Douglas stands over the vanquished Mike Tyson, February 10, 1990.

1994, it happened—the former heavyweight champion collapsed in a diabetic coma. He was 33 years old, a man who should have been in the prime of his life, but there he was, in a hospital emergency room, the prime of his life slipping away. "When I got out of the hospital, I got back on my feet," Douglas said. "It hit me. I needed to get a goal, something to get me back where I was."

Douglas may never get back where he was, but only because the destination seemed so unreachable the first time around. After all, how many times can you be on top of the world, the piece of real estate where Douglas resided after defeating Tyson in 1990? Douglas was such a huge underdog that the Las Vegas casinos refused to post odds on the fight, but he did it, knocking out Tyson in the 10th round to win the world heavyweight title—one of the biggest upsets in boxing history. The new champion felt like a kid, hugging his title belt as if it were a teddy bear.

Not bad for a guy who seemed like a reluctant warrior, a guy so lackadaisical that his own father did not believe in him. And who could blame

the old man? Billy Douglas was a middleweight contender in the 1970s, and he tried to mold his son into the kind of fighter he had been—a monster who could make a street fight look like a friendly debate. But "Buster" rebelled. He saw himself as a boxer, a Picasso with padded gloves, and the old man got frustrated. "I never knew if 'Buster' really wanted to be a fighter," Billy Douglas said. "I just didn't know if he had the determination."

On one glorious night, Douglas proved his father—and all his other critics—wrong. He battered Tyson, the invincible champion, by flooring him with a combination so sweet and pure that it looked like a shadow-boxing routine. Tyson, who landed on his black silk trunks, scrambled around the ring on all fours, searching for the mouthpiece that had tumbled out of his mouth from the final punch. He searched and searched, and the referee counted and counted, but the referee reached 10 before the fighter reached his mouthpiece. And so ended one of the biggest upsets in boxing history.

"I feel excited again," Douglas said after getting out of the hospital. And no wonder: Douglas launched his comeback about two years after collapsing into the diabetic coma. The ex-champion lost more than 150 pounds (68kg), and the glorious boxer he used to be reemerged from layers of fat—and years of abuse. He knocked out Tony LaRosa on June 22, 1996, his first bout since the disastrous loss to Holyfield on October 25, 1990. Then he won five more fights, two of them by knockout, before suffering a setback as critical as the defeat against Holyfield almost ten years before: a shocking loss to Lou Savarese, who knocked out the ex-champion in the 1st round. "I didn't take it seriously enough," Douglas said. "I didn't train the way I should have. I know what I did wrong. I learned my lesson."

Douglas will keep fighting, and while he may never recover from the loss to Savarese, he has recaptured something more significant than his heavyweight crown—his life. And that may represent the single greatest comeback in boxing history. "I'm excited, but it's not just about boxing," Douglas said before fighting Savarese. "It's about living, it's about life, because I almost left it. I didn't feel good about myself back then, but now I feel great about myself. I feel like a very fortunate young man."

ous months, Douglas was a bona fide hero, the man who conquered the "bad guy" of boxing—heavyweight champion Mike Tyson. He knocked out Tyson on February 11 in Tokyo, scoring one of the biggest upsets in boxing history.

If Douglas savored his victory, who could blame him? He was living a dream. When he was growing up in Columbus, Ohio, most of his friends found their heroes in comic books. Not Buster. He found one in real life—his father, Billy Douglas. Buster began boxing when he was 10 years old, following in the footsteps of his dad, a middleweight contender in the 1970s. Billy, who worked at an auto parts factory during his fighting days, never encouraged his son to box; he didn't have to. Watching his father fight, Buster felt so much pride that he wanted to fight, too

"It was exciting," the son recalled. "He took me to some of his fights. I even went to Madison Square Garden to watch him box. It was wild."

Yet, while Buster loved his father, he did not want to be like him—at least not in the ring. The old man was a brawler, and Buster wanted to box. He wanted to win, but he did not want to get hurt on his way to victory.

"I just had that in me—attack, attack, attack," Billy said, "but Buster was completely different. He was a boxer, not a puncher."

They had their rough moments, moments so emotionally draining that Buster considered retiring from boxing. It came to a head on May 30, 1987, when Buster met Tony Tucker, then the International Boxing Federation heavyweight champion. Buster was ahead on points going into the 10th round. Then he walked into a right hand that rendered his brilliant boxing in the nine other rounds irrelevant. He went down—down and out.

"James told me after the fight that he was sitting on the stool after the ninth round and decided he just didn't want to win the fight," said John Johnson, who

Julio Cesar Chavez was a calm, efficient boxer, a master at wearing opponents down with repeated blows to the body. His strategic method enabled him to put together a tremendous wins record over the course of his career.

managed Douglas. "He just gave up. All the distractions with his father had gotten to him."

If Buster gave up on that fight, however, he did not give up on his career. He worked his way up the rankings, earning a shot at Tyson. He won with a spectacular display of boxing and punching, and it made the old man proud.

It would not last. Douglas lost the title in his first defense, to Evander Holyfield, on October 25, 1990, in Las Vegas, Nevada. It was a shocking defeat, as devastating as the Tyson bout had been exhilarating. And it left Douglas with a curious legacy. He was not one of the greatest heavyweights in history—he would be hard pressed to crack the Top 20—but he enjoyed one of the most magical nights a fighter has ever experienced.

## Julio Cesar Chavez

For almost twenty years, Julio Cesar Chavez threw left hook after left hook, punches that damaged more livers than all the tequila in Guadalajara. They called him "el gran campeon Mexicano"—the great Mexican champion—but he was more than that. He was the greatest fighter of his generation, a man who won eighty-seven fights, seventy-five of them by knockout, before suffering the first blemish on his record: the controversial draw against Pernell "Sweetpea" Whitaker on September 11, 1993, in San Antonio.

How did he do it? He was not flashy or powerful, but he was nonetheless an exciting fighter. Chavez was a model of economy, every punch as short and sweet as a hatchet stroke. And he was smart, too. Chavez maintained the delicate balance that every great fighter must master—the line between fury and tranquillity. He turned his fights into sparring sessions, exercises in methodical destruction.

Like most great fighters, he set up his combinations with a single punch, but it was not the jab. It was the left hook to the liver, a punch that left most of his opponents wondering where he concealed the sledgehammers. The answer? Inside his leather gloves. "If you go downstairs, to the body, you can take away a man's will and desire," Chavez said.

A superb fighter for almost seven years, Chavez became a great one—at least in the eyes of the boxing

carried out step by step—first the body, then the head. He was amazingly accurate, and he seemed to know where a punch would inflict the most pain, the most damage. Just ask Rosario, who looked like a gargoyle after the fight, his face bruised and swollen, a man who was beaten long before the referee stopped the punishment. "The guy just knows how to fight," said George Benton, who trained Whitaker. "It's as simple as that. The guy knows how to fight."

Julio Cesar Chavez celebrates after winning the final rounds to defeat David Kamau on September 16, 1995, by decision. At this point in his career, Chavez was just beginning to show signs of being mortal.

world—on November 21, 1987, when he won the lightweight title with an 11th-round knockout of Edwin Rosario. It was a strange, almost remarkable fight, because Chavez took the heavier punches throughout the bout; he just did not take as many as Rosario did. Chavez remained calm and composed throughout the match, as if the demolition had to be

One of ten children born to Rodolfo and Isabelita Chavez, he grew up in Culiacan, Mexico, a working-class town in the state of Sinaloa. The father was a brakeman for the railroad, but the pay was so bad that the children sometimes ate boiled weeds for dinner. He supplemented his income by selling the medicine that the Mexican government supplied to poor families.

"Thank God I became a boxer," Chavez said. "Now I can help my family with money."

Chavez turned pro when he was 18, about eight years after walking into a gym for the first time. He fought his first thirty-three bouts in Mexico, sometimes earning as little as $6 per fight. The young fighter won all of them, thirty-one by knockout. "My older brothers were boxers," Chavez said. "One day, one of my brothers lost a fight. I was so angry, not at my brother, but at the world. I hated losing. I hated the thought of losing. I was 10 years old, and I promised myself that I would never lose." Later in his career, the greatest fighter of his era would lose that status, passing the mantle, stubbornly and grudgingly, to younger, stronger fighters. First was the draw with Whitaker, a fight that most observers felt Whitaker had won. Chavez fought his fight, calmly pursuing his opponent throughout the match, but to no avail. Whitaker was too fast, too elusive. Then came Frankie Randall, who dropped the great fighter en route to a decision on January 29, 1994, in Las Vegas. And then came perhaps the toughest opponent of his career—Oscar De La Hoya, who fought Chavez in 1996 and 1998. De La Hoya stopped him both times, conquering him with speed, power, and youth. The last fight forced Chavez, proud but beaten, to contemplate retirement. "He was a great champion, but his time is past," De La Hoya said. "It's time for him to retire."

## Pernell Whitaker

If Julio Cesar Chavez was calm and composed in the ring, Pernell "Sweetpea" Whitaker was loud and brash, a fighter whose style owed more to Abbott and

ABOVE: Julio Cesar Chavez ducks a left thrown by Pernell Whitaker during their September 11, 1993, match-up in San Antonio, Texas. The fight was scored a draw, but many observers felt Whitaker had won.

Costello than to Leonard and Hearns. Does that sound crazy? Well, Whitaker looked crazy. He fought like a cartoon character, jumping on the ropes, sticking out his tongue, and clapping at his virtuosity in the ring. "I've screamed at him to remain focused in the ring, but he does what he wants to do," said Lou Duva, who helped guide the champion to world titles in four weight classes: lightweight, junior welterweight, welterweight, and junior middleweight. "It makes me mad. I don't know why he does it. I think he's so dominating in the ring that things get monotonous for him. He gets bored, and he thinks he has to spice things up."

And who could blame him? Whitaker recoiled at the thought of getting hit, but it was not out of fear—or even concern—for his own safety. It was just that Whitaker, who took as much pride in his defense as he did in his offense, was so elusive that he could not even imagine getting hit. He fought entire bouts, punching and retreating, punching and retreating, without losing a single round, sometimes without absorbing a single punch, making his decisions seem as definitive as knockouts.

Whitaker was a smooth, elegant boxer, his footwork so dainty that he looked like a ballerina, but there was still the clownish streak, the one that riled his trainers. Who could forget his battle against Roger Mayweather on March 28, 1987, when he did everything but throw a cream pie at his opponent? He slipped behind Mayweather during one of the clinches, pulling down Mayweather's trunks and running away—an antic that left the referee looking like a

schoolteacher trying to discipline the class clown. Whitaker went on to win the fight, but the lapse of concentration caused him to suffer the first knockdown of his career. "Nobody knows if he can take a punch," Chavez said. "We'll find out."

Chavez was wrong. Chavez tried to find out—

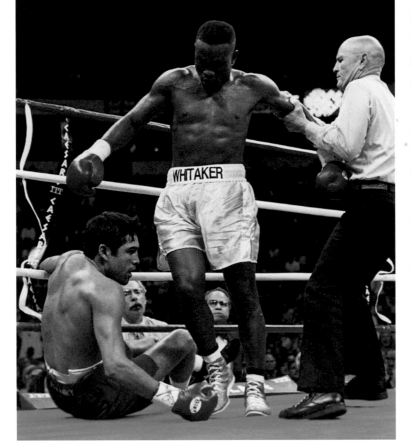

ABOVE: Much like Willie Pep, Pernell Whitaker was a defensive specialist. Alas, it was Whitaker's misfortune to arrive at a time of excellent competition in his division, especially in the person of Oscar De La Hoya. Whitaker met his match in De La Hoya, seen here on the mat, who wrested the welterweight title from Whitaker with a decision in this April 12, 1997, fight.

relentlessly, if not desperately—but, try as he might, he missed punch after punch, punishing the air, not the man in front of him. The two men fought to a draw, a decision that was booed by most of the sixty thousand fans in the Alamodome in San Antonio. "You saw the fight," Whitaker said afterward. "Everybody knows I won."

The public bestowed upon Whitaker what the judges had denied him—a victory. It may have been a symbolic victory, but it did not matter to Whitaker, because the boxing world crowned him with the mythical title that Chavez had held for so long—greatest fighter in the world, pound for pound. And he relished it. "It's the only title that means anything to me," he said.

The welterweight fighter held the mythical title of champion until April 12, 1997, when he met Oscar De La Hoya, the only American athlete to win a gold medal in the 1992 Olympics. Whitaker sneered at his young opponent, calling him "Liberace," a reference to the gaggle of female fans who screamed and shrieked at "the Golden Boy" during the prefight weigh-in at Caesars Palace in Las Vegas. Liberace? Maybe, but if this was Liberace, it was Liberace from hell, a guy who would happily smash you in the face with one of his candelabra.

Whitaker tried to elude the young fighter, bobbing and dipping throughout the bout, but De La Hoya was not Chavez. "The Golden Boy" refused to pursue him calmly and patiently, letting precious rounds slip away in the process, as Chavez had done four years before. No, De La Hoya boxed furiously, forcing a fight that Whitaker tried to avoid. He scored a decision over Whitaker, and this time there was no controversy, although Whitaker tried to create one, saying he had gotten robbed again. Wrong. De La Hoya beat him fair and square, wresting the mythical title of the greatest fighter in the world, pound for pound, from the proud virtual champion. "Whitaker can say all he wants, but I'm the welterweight champion," De La Hoya said, calmly holding up his championship belt.

## Evander Holyfield

It was Body Beautiful versus Body Bountiful, and the beauty won. The two men fought on October 25, 1990, in Las Vegas, but they waged their own battles long before that, in the arena where all fights are won or lost—the gym. Punish yourself in the gym, the credo goes, and you will punish your opponent in the ring. Evander Holyfield punished himself; James "Buster" Douglas did not. So Body Beautiful beat Body Bountiful, knocking him out in the 3rd round to capture the heavyweight championship of the world. Score one for dedication and hard work—Holyfield weighed 208 pounds (94kg), 38 pounds (17kg) less than his pudgy opponent.

Who would have guessed that Body Beautiful was once Body Pitiful, a short, scrawny kid who agonized on the bench of his high school football team in Atlanta? It was more than twenty years ago, but the memories seem sharp and vivid because Holyfield cherishes the failures as much as he does the successes; they make him stronger, more determined, reminding him that he was not born the heavyweight champion of the world. So, yes, he treasures the past, and he keeps that little guy—so distant, yet so near—close to his heart. "I know I'm still the little guy," Holyfield said.

RIGHT: Evander Holyfield pounds Dwight Muhammad Qawi to capture the cruiser weight title on June 12, 1986. Holyfield has always been in top physical shape at every stage of his career.

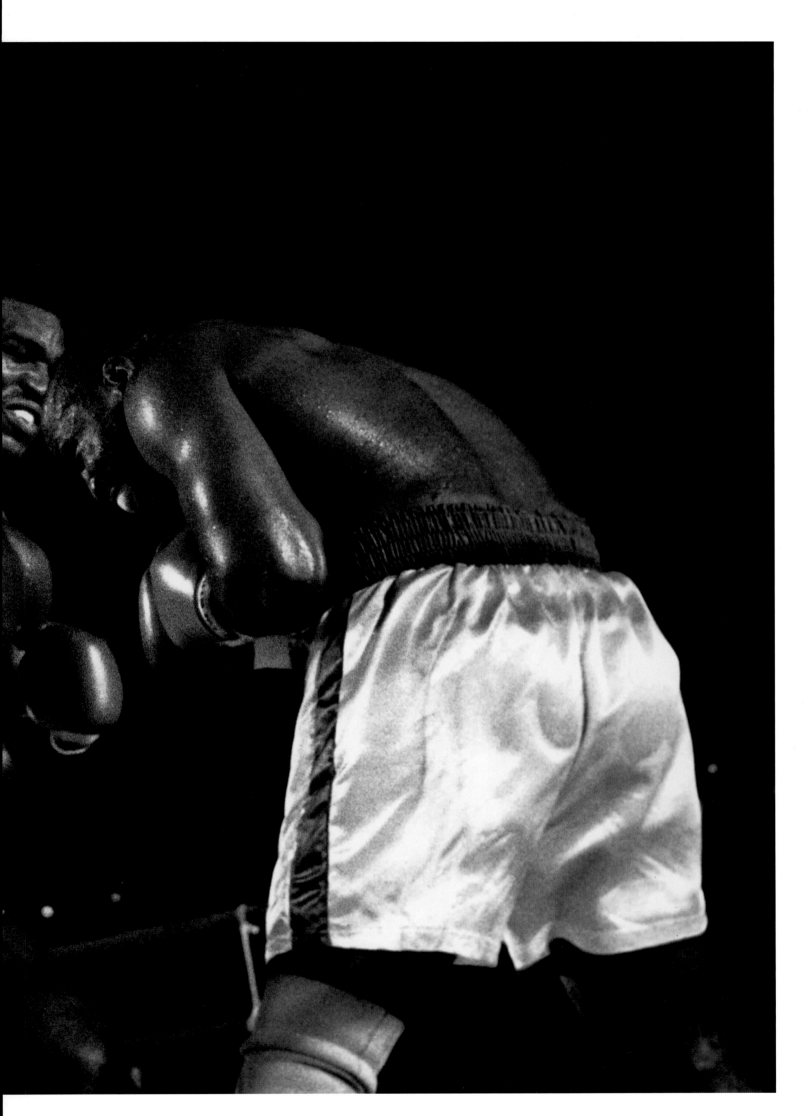

"But, if I were a coach, I'd rather have a big heart than a big man."

A 5-foot-4-inch (163cm), 115-pound (52kg) cornerback, the high school junior abandoned football in 1978, the season on the bench having bruised his ego as well as his butt. He turned to boxing, a sport he would grow to love. Here was a competition where every youngster, no matter how short or light, had an equal chance to succeed—or fail. And as the youngster grew, so did his love for the sport. He compiled an amateur record of 160-14, with 75 knockouts, and won a bronze medal in the light heavyweight division at the 1980 Olympics in Los Angeles. Not bad for the scrawny kid who was overlooked by his high school football coach. "You know, I was picked on so much when I was small that I still have that little-guy mentality," Holyfield said.

Holyfield maintained that attitude as a professional, winning the world cruiser weight title in his twelfth professional fight—a stirring decision over Dwight Muhammad Qawi, formerly Dwight Braxton, "the Camden Buzzsaw." The champion defended his title five times, every time with sensational knockouts, and he became known as the greatest cruiser weight in history. So what? It was like calling Herbert Hoover the greatest president to come out of West Branch, Iowa.

ABOVE: Holyfield dodges a blow by champion Buster Douglas during a title bout on October 25, 1990. Holyfield triumphed, winning the heavyweight title from Douglas scant months after Douglas had stunned the boxing world by knocking out the seemingly invincible Mike Tyson. Holyfield's victory set the stage for one of the more unusual rivalries in boxing history, which would see Tyson try to reclaim the heavyweight crown in a couple of highly publicized bouts.

ABOVE: Evander Holyfield and Riddick Bowe had one of the classic rivalries of heavyweight boxing. The gigantic Bowe proved a good match for the athletic (though much smaller) Holyfield, who won one and lost two of their three bouts. Still, Holyfield had the greater overall career, going on to best Mike Tyson and join Ali as the only other three-time heavyweight champion. This fight, their first, took place on November 13, 1992.

Holyfield did not need that kind of praise, so like Michael Spinks before him, he moved on and up—to the heavyweight division. "It's definitely a challenge," said Tim Hallmark, the fitness guru who was hired to turn Holyfield into a heavyweight. "But, then, it's always a challenge when you talk about putting weight on, because you're talking about a major change. You might do it with a person off the street very easily. But with an athlete, you just don't want to put weight on; you want to put weight on and, at the same time, have him perform as well as he possibly can."

While most boxers confine their workouts to jogging and gym sessions, Holyfield ran, swam, sparred, and lifted weights during three workouts a day, six days a week—a brutal pace that he thought would make him a brutal force. He was right. Holyfield knocked out Douglas for the title, a fight he seemed destined to win from the moment he stepped into the ring, when he skipped from corner to corner in what looked like a victory dance.

When he met Riddick Bowe on November 13, 1992, in Las Vegas, he was the little guy again, dwarfed by a man whose size matched his talent. The challenger weighed 235 pounds (107kg), 30 pounds (14kg) more than the champion, and it showed. Bowe towered over Holyfield during the prefight instructions, displaying his enormous advantages before the fight even started—30 pounds (14kg) in weight, 3 inches (8cm) in height, 4 inches (10cm) in reach. He made the title holder look like an urchin sitting on a curb—a vivid reminder of why he referred to Holyfield as "that little guy you all call the champion." They would not call him champion for long; Bowe scored a 12-round decision over his brave but overmatched opponent.

The two men fought two more times, forming the greatest trilogy in the heavyweight division since the Ali-Frazier wars of the 1970s. Holyfield won the second fight and Bowe the third, fights that seemed to define the careers of both fighters, just as the Ali-Frazier fights had done two decades earlier. But Holyfield did not need Bowe, a foil to serve as a measuring stick for his heart and skill, because he emerged as a great fighter against another opponent—Mike Tyson.

They met on November 9, 1996, in Las Vegas, and when the opening bell rang, Tyson displayed the same urgency he had shown throughout most of his career.

He threw the first punch of the fight, a wide, arching right hand that sent his opponent into the ropes. Holyfield backpedaled, his hands shooting up awkwardly, but he did not go down, and Tyson seemed shocked. He became even more shocked, emotionally and physically, because for every punch Tyson threw, Holyfield threw three, sometimes four, not all of them landing, but all of them telling Tyson that finally— finally—here was a man who would stand up to him. Holyfield stopped him in the 11th round. "Holyfield's a good fighter," Tyson said. "And I want a rematch."

The challenger got his wish eight months later but, unable to overcome the new champion with his fists, he resorted to his teeth, biting his opponent on both ears in the 3rd round. Referee Mills Lane disqualified Tyson, and Holyfield emerged with another victory over the man he had branded a bully. "When you try to foul to get out of a fight, it's not showing too much courage," Holyfield said afterward. So Holyfield, the man who had given his heart and soul to boxing since his youth, ended up giving a piece of his ear as well.

## Roy Jones

When he is attending a fight rather than engaging in one, Roy Jones swaggers up and down the arena, a proud champion in fancy duds—clothes that look like the subject of a Peter Max painting, bright and vivid and colorful. But if he is gaudy and flashy outside the ring, it is nothing compared to how he looks inside the ring, where he is one of the most dominant fighters of the day. He may not be the greatest fighter in the world—but he is the most outrageously talented, combining so much speed and power that, like Ali before him, he gets away with his mechanical flaws. Or are they mechanical flaws? "Everyone thinks I'm an unorthodox fighter, but I'm not," Jones said. "I'm an orthodox fighter. People just don't know what they're looking at."

Perhaps, but Jones makes the unorthodox look orthodox because he is so smooth and graceful. But

RIGHT: Roy Jones unleashes a left to the body of Otis Grant on November 14, 1998. Jones won this fight by TKO in the 10th. Jones seems to be a boxer for the ages, a combination of blinding speed, incredible athleticism, and awesome power. If he has one flaw, it might be his technique, though some would say it is simply that he has his own style.

make no mistake: he does everything wrong; he just gets away with it because of his enormous talent. Jones keeps his hands low, leads with his right, throws punches off the wrong foot—flaws that would send most trainers into therapy. Most trainers, but not Eddie Futch. "He may be the most talented fighter since Sugar Ray Robinson," Futch said.

Jones displayed those skills on November 18, 1994, in Las Vegas, capturing the super middleweight title with a unanimous decision over James Toney, then one of the greatest fighters in the world. It was a fight of contrasts,

chin, a target as inviting as a piñata. He seemed out of punching range—at least to everyone but the challenger—but he was not. The left hook came from about 10 inches (25cm) away, a blow as unlikely as it was powerful. Toney crumpled to the floor, near his own corner, as the challenger tried to hit him again on his way down. Toney beat the 10-count, but Jones maintained his peculiar brand of pressure, brutal yet elegant, on his way to a unanimous decision. "God blessed me with a lot of foot speed and hand speed," Jones said. "And I figured that was the way to go. I

ABOVE: Roy Jones pummels the midsection of James Toney, at the time considered one of the most dangerous fighters in his division, en route to capturing the super middleweight title on November 18, 1994. OPPOSITE: Roy Jones celebrates his emphatic 1st-round knockout of Montell Griffin on August 7, 1997, regaining the world light heavyweight title and avenging an earlier loss to Griffin in the process.

and the differences emerged before the opening bell. Toney, the champion, entered the ring with a ski cap and a menacing glare, while Jones chose a more elegant outfit—a white silk tuxedo with gold vest and black bow tie. The champion walked up to the challenger, calmly but defiantly, trying to stare him down before the prefight instructions. Jones refused to be intimidated.

In a stunning 3rd round, Toney committed an error—a stupid and uncharacteristic error. Jones showboated, shuffling his feet and pumping his fists into the air, and the champion responded with his own act of bravado. Toney dropped his hands and stuck out his

could feel his power. He's a very strong puncher, and I've been taught to counter strong punchers."

Jones looked unbeatable, and he was—unless the opponent was Jones himself. He lost to Montell Griffin on March 21, 1977, when he was disqualified for an illegal blow. Griffin took a punch to the jaw after dropping to one knee in an attempt to avoid one of those lightning-bolt combinations from the champion. Griffin was awarded the world light heavyweight title, a crown Jones regained with a 1st-round knockout five months later. "The only man who can beat Roy Jones is Roy Jones," said Jones. How true.

# THE BOSSES    3

**A boxer solidly constructed, intelligently directed, and soundly motivated is bound to go a long way.**

**—A.J. Liebling in *The Sweet Science***

They called it Champs Gym, and it was like any gym in the United States—a place with the camaraderie of a tavern, the lighting of a coal mine, and the ambience of a bus station. It was located above an automobile body shop, and it was hard to tell who did the heavier pounding, the mechanics or the boxers. Fight posters lined the walls, and exposed wires snaked out of the sockets, creating a hazard that all the pugs ignored. Champs had class.

When Champs was empty it looked small, but when the fighters started to arrive it looked even smaller, shrinking to the size of a broom closet. Fighters jockeyed for position like basketball players in the paint, keeping a wary eye for unintentional blows from buddies who were shadowboxing. The boxers repeated their routines day after day without bumping into each other—which qualified as a minor miracle. "This is how gyms should be," said Al Fennell, who trained former junior middleweight champion Robert "Bam Bam" Hines.

It was a great place, a kind of hideaway, as long as you were not one of the pugs getting whacked in the ring. The neighborhood men used to go there every day, most of them old guys, as eager and enthusiastic as the young fighters they watched. They sat in chairs lined against the wall, and their discussions were like those common in barber shops—spirited debates about the best fighters in the world, both today and yesterday.

Champs was located in Philadelphia, one of the greatest boxing towns in the world—perhaps the greatest. But there are gyms like Champs everywhere. Oh, the quality of fighters may not be the same at gyms in Tulsa or Canton or Poughkeepsie, but the environments are the same, with a grim charm that only fight people can appreciate. Take the crummy old gym in Secaucus, New Jersey, where Chuck Wepner trained. They called him "the Bayonne Bleeder," and for good reason; every man he fought had razors for fists, leaving him with a face only a plastic surgeon could love. *Screw* magazine once ran a full-page photograph of him; his brows were slashed, his cheeks swollen, his lips split from here to Trenton. The caption stated, "Now THIS is obscene." Wepner bled in the gym, too, and his blood ended up everywhere, on the canvas, on the floors, on the walls—perhaps the most primitive display of splatter art in the world.

**ABOVE** Up-and-coming female boxer Lucia Rijker (right) gets some advice from coach Freddie Roach during her March 25, 1998, fight against Marcela Avna at Foxwoods Casino, in Ledyard, Connecticut. **OPPOSITE:** Jack Dempsey was one of the greatest boxers of the first half of the twentieth century; it's amazing to think that he came along just a little more than twenty years after the end of the brawling, bareknuckle era. Here, Dempsey takes a playful stab at the punching bag in Mac Levy's Gym at Madison Square Garden while legendary promoter and impresario Tex Rickard looks on. Rickard was at least in part responsible for the emergence of boxing from the dark ages of the pre–Marquess of Queensberry era and its rise to immense popularity.

If gyms are great environments, it is only because they house interesting, colorful people. Interesting people are those who speak their minds, and boxing people are among the most open and genuine in the world. Oh, they will lie to you, all right, but it as honest as lying ever gets. If that sounds crazy, consider the case of promoter Bob Arum who, once trapped in an inconsistency, said, "Yesterday, I was lying. Today, I'm telling the truth." Gyms are full of people like that—not just the fighters, but also the managers, the trainers, and, when they want to check in on their investments, the promoters.

## The Trainers

### *Eddie Futch*

It was one of those hot, steamy gyms that turn your pores into water spouts, but one thing made Eddie Futch sweat more than the environment: the thought of sparring with his boyhood friend, Joe Louis, who had just knocked out James J. Braddock to become the heavyweight champion of the world. Scary. It was the summer of 1937, in Detroit, Michigan, and Futch was 27 years old—young enough to be adventurous, but old enough to know that adventurousness could land you in a hospital ward. Smart man, Eddie Futch. Yes, he refused to spar with Louis, and yes, he lived to fight—and, more importantly, train—another day.

The boxing world is grateful. Futch became one of the greatest trainers in boxing history, perhaps the greatest, because he saw fights in slow motion, dissecting them from the corner as if the live action were a fight tape, the drama unfolding slowly, punch by punch, until the keys to victory became clear to the wise, little man at ringside. Then he would climb the steps to the ring, slowly and gingerly in his later years, and discuss the strategy with his fighter. Yes, discuss the strategy. Boxing is a brutal, chaotic sport, but Futch was a calm, gentle man, so there were no theatrics in the corner, no fireworks, no cheerleading. He was emotional, but his emotion came from his inner confidence and his keen intelligence; his fighters knew that and respected him for it. "I've had a lot of trainers," said Marlon Starling, the former welter-

Over the years, trainer Eddie Futch guided many boxers to success, including heavyweight champion Riddick Bowe (to whom Futch is speaking in this photograph).

weight champion of the world. "But Eddie Futch is the only one I've had who knows more about boxing than I do."

When Futch discussed boxing, he was almost professorial. The ring was his classroom, and more than fifteen of his students graduated to world titles, including Marlon Starling, Joe Frazier, Alexis Arguello, Larry Holmes, Michael Spinks, and Riddick Bowe. They were all different, from the elegance of Arguello to the herky-jerky moves of Spinks, but Futch molded all of them into superb fighters, improving their styles with a new move here, a new dip there. He enhanced; he did not dismantle. "No matter how good a fighter is, you can turn his strengths into weaknesses," said Futch, now 88. "Take the fight between Michael Spinks and Gerry Cooney, for example. Cooney had a tremendous left hook, a tremendous left hook, but a straight right beats a left hook every time."

Spinks knocked out Cooney in the 5th round on June 15, 1987, in Atlantic City—the "War at the Shore" that Spinks won with, yes, the straight right. "I don't think there was a better trainer around than my good friend Eddie Futch," said Angelo Dundee, himself one of the greatest trainers in boxing history. Futch was also a compassionate man. "I don't want Marvis hurt," he told Larry Holmes, then the heavyweight champion, before he fought Marvis Frazier on November 25, 1983, in Las Vegas. Marvis Frazier was the son of former heavyweight champion Joe Frazier, whom Futch had also trained. Futch loved both Joe and his son, and he did not want to see either of them get hurt, one physically, the other emotionally. Holmes knocked out the kid in the 1st round. "I want you to get him out of there as fast as you can," Futch had told Holmes.

Futch became a trainer in the 1940s, but his fighters were drawing so little attention that he had to hold down two other jobs, as a hotel busboy and a postal clerk. Then one of his fighters, Lester Felton, won a 10-round decision over the highly regarded Kid Gavilan, who would go on to win the welterweight title, and the boxing world started to take notice of the trainer from Detroit. He stopped moonlighting. "It was a hard road, but that one fight put me on the right path," he said.

One of three children reared in Detroit, Futch preferred basketball over boxing, playing guard in a league sponsored by the YMCA. But one day, he did something that would change his life: he bought a speed bag—one of those big, yellow models that looked more like a heavy bag. "I was punching it one day, and the Y director saw me," Futch recalled. "He was impressed, so he invited me down to the boxing club to work out. I kept saying no, but he kept encouraging me." Futch finally said yes, and when he entered the dark, sweaty gym for the first time, he was fascinated by the fighters, the workouts, even the noise—the rhythmic tapping of the speed bags, the thud of the medicine balls slamming into bellies, the whoosh and whirr of the fighters skipping rope in front of full-length mirrors. The youngster was hooked. He did not realize it, not yet, but he was hooked. "I began to love boxing," he recalled. "One of the boxers in the club was Joe Louis, and I got to know him well."

Futch won city and national tournaments, ultimately capturing the National Amateur Athletic Union championship in 1934. "I loved boxing, but I thought I would make a good teacher of boxing," he said. "I wanted to train other fighters." After Louis won the title, he returned to Detroit, hoping to spar with the boyhood friend who would become one of the greatest trainers in boxing history. "I had sparred with him before he turned professional, but now he was bigger and stronger, and his punches could paralyze you," said Futch, then a junior welterweight. "I said, 'No, I'm not going to work for you, Joe.' He said, 'Eddie, you're going to get paid $10 a round.' That was very good money back then, but I said, 'Yeah, I can use it to pay my doctor's bills.'"

Louis persisted, saying he wanted to spar with his friend to measure his progress as a pro. Futch thought he was the one who would be measured—for a coffin. He said no again, this time more emphatically. "I ended up keeping time for the workouts," Futch said. "He knocked out two of the sparring partners." Afterward, Futch went up to one of the sparring partners and asked, "Are you okay?"

"Yeah, I'm fine," the sparring partner responded. "Why?"

"Well, you got hit pretty hard," Futch said.

"What do you mean?" the guy asked.

"Do you remember stepping into the ring?" Futch asked.

"Yeah," the sparring partner said.

"Do you remember stepping out of the ring?" Futch asked.

"No," the guy said.

"Oh-oh," Futch said. "You got hit harder than I thought."

And to think it could have been Futch. But Futch was too smart to spar with Louis because he exercised the same intelligence he used as a trainer. He retired in 1997, but you can ask his old fighters—and their opponents—about that intelligence.

### Angelo Dundee

Leaning across the ropes, close enough to land or absorb a left hook, Angelo Dundee looks like a choreographer, directing his fighters to dip here, bend there. One, two, three, step. Four, five, six, punch. Is this a gym or a dance studio? The answer is both, because

like all great trainers, Dundee knows that boxers fight with their legs as well as their hands, their lower bodies putting them in position for their upper bodies to attack—or avoid getting attacked. If boxing is a dance—and it is—Dundee understands the steps as well as anyone, because he trained two of the greatest dancers in history—Muhammad Ali and Sugar Ray Leonard.

"Leonard was a great kid, a great fighter, and nobody's ever had the impact on boxing that Muhammad Ali has," Dundee, 76, said.

While Ali and Leonard were outrageously talented, with fights that captured the attention of the world, Dundee remembers the quiet moments, too: "Ali was still Cassius Clay at the time, and he was going to fight at an arena in Louisville. It was about three hours before the fight, and he asked me if we could go down to the arena. I didn't know what he wanted to do, but I said, 'Sure.'"

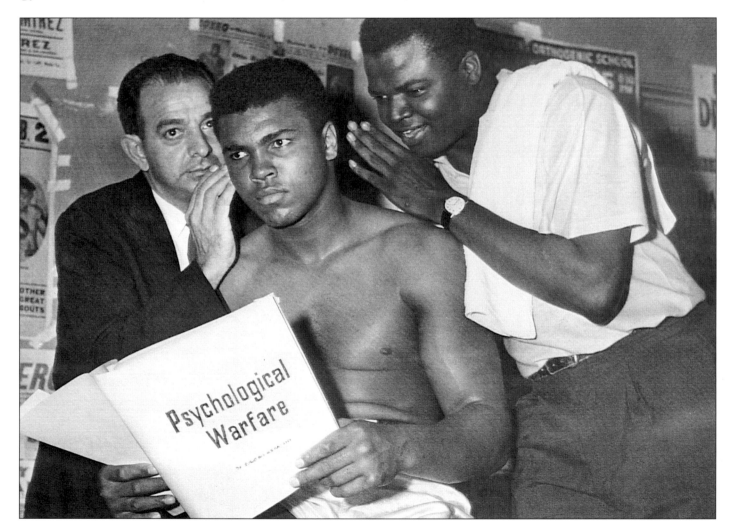

ABOVE: A young Cassius Clay carefully studies a handbook on psychological warfare on February 6, 1964, while trainer Angelo Dundee (left) and motivator Drew Brown refine those principles by whispering into the boxer's ears. As Muhammad Ali, he would go on to add his own chapters to the annals of psychological warfare. OPPOSITE: Trainer Angelo Dundee uses a clenched fist to demonstrate a point to Sugar Ray Leonard between rounds in a middleweight title bout against Marvelous Marvin Hagler in 1987. A credit to Dundee's abilities, Leonard won the fight with a split decision.

When trainers and fighters arrived at the dressing room in the arena, Ali started shadowboxing...and shadowboxing...and shadowboxing. Every once in a while, he would stand in front of a full-length mirror, smiling and preening as the sweat slid down his face like thin oil, and then he would resume shadowboxing, his fists punishing the air in the hot, stale dressing room. It went on for three hours. Why? It seemed crazy, but there was a reason for the insanity. Ali, the self-proclaimed greatest of all time, was a master of exploiting fear—not his own, but that of his opponents. But he felt fear, too, felt the dread and anxiety of stepping into the ring, where one left hook can bruise both your jaw and your ego. And on that day, in that dressing room, Ali shadowboxed furiously, and his fear evaporated along with his sweat. "I mean, I've heard of fighters warming up 30 minutes before the fight," Dundee said. "But this sucker warmed up for three hours. He would dance and shout, 'Look at me, ain't I pretty?' For three hours." But the workout relaxed Ali, and Dundee loves fighters who are relaxed. "You've got to have fun," he said. "I like a light situation, because I think you get the best out of that situation. Hey, you've got to be happy."

A native of south Philadelphia, Dundee roamed the streets that Sylvester Stallone would make famous in his *Rocky* films. Dundee was a chubby kid, the constant target of cruel jokes, and he decided to build himself a new body. He began to train as a fighter at the Mason Hall gym in south Philly, overcoming a significant problem in an ingenious manner. His father, a stern but loving Italian immigrant, disapproved of boxing, so the youngster, born Angelo Mirenda, trained under the name of Angelo Dundee, a false surname an older brother had used before him. "Why the name Dundee?" said the trainer, who has since changed his name legally. "Well, there were some Italian fighters who had used the name earlier. There was a Vince Lazarro who changed his name to Dundee, and he became middleweight champ in 1933. Now, kids come up to me and ask, 'Are you related to Crocodile Dundee?'"

After serving in the Air Corps during World War II, Dundee moved to New York, then the boxing capital of the world. He lived in a hotel across the street from Madison Square Garden, a piece of real estate that he regarded as heaven, and he watched the great

trainers of his day—Ray Arcel, Whitey Bimstein, and Charlie Goldman. He picked up tricks from each man, learning how to wrap hands, handle cuts, and boost the confidence of a seemingly beaten fighter. Dundee the apprentice became Dundee the master. "All of my fighters have been special," Dundee said. "It takes a special man to climb into the ring." And it takes a special man to train them. Dundee has worked with eleven world champions, either as a trainer or a cut man, including Carmen Basilio, who became his first title holder when he stopped Tony Demarco in the 11th round for the welterweight crown on June 10, 1955, in New York. "Basilio bled easily," Dundee said. "He'd bleed at press conferences. I said that once to some reporters, and he didn't like it. But he got over it."

Unlike his good friend Eddie Futch, who was calm and composed before and after a fight, Dundee was a different man once the bell rang—a man who could make the case of Dr. Jekyll and Mr. Hyde look like a gentle mood swing. He displayed that attitude on May 30, 1987, when he worked the corner for Pinklon Thomas, who was facing Mike Tyson, then the heavyweight champion of the world. The ring doctor tried to examine Thomas, who had absorbed a vicious barrage to the head, between rounds. Dundee bristled, afraid that this intrusion would make his fighter think he was hurt, whether he was or not, and he began screaming at the doctor. "My wife was sitting at ringside, and she got scared for me," Dundee said.

Tyson stopped Thomas in the 6th round, but the trainer-physician bout was almost as exciting. "The chairman of the athletic commission got me by the arm and said, 'That's a $500 fine,'" Dundee recalled. "I kept yelling. Then he said, '$1,000.' I said, 'Amen.' But I gladly paid it."

Dundee gladly paid it because the alternative would have been worse: sitting quietly while his fighter needed his help. "I never know what I'm going to do," he said. "It's always an ad-lib with me. Naturally, I'm looking to win. I'm not a good loser. I don't like to see my fighter lose. The idea is win, win, win."

OPPOSITE: George Benton tapes Evander Holyfield's hands while trainer Lou Duva (second from right) and strength coach Tim Hallmark look on. Having been a fighter of some promise himself, not to mention a gentleman in every sense of the word, Benton easily made the transition to successful trainer.

## George Benton

When George Benton fought as a middleweight from 1949 to 1970, compiling a record of 67-12-1, he was the consummate professional—a defensive genius who could punch. Oh yes, he could punch. His right hand was a two-by-four, and whenever he starched a pug, he

Holyfield. "It's a little easier to break through in boxing nowadays," said Benton, 65. "Back then, a champion could pick the guys he wanted to fight. That's not so much the case anymore."

If Benton was elegant as a fighter, he was also elegant as a trainer. He attended training sessions in a suit and tie with a silk handkerchief blossoming from his coat pocket, as if the gym were a fancy restaurant

would return to his corner slowly and deliberately, as if he had done nothing more strenuous than pick up the mail. Benton was cool; it was part of his code.

Benton was cool in the corner, too. As a middleweight, he never got the opportunity to fight for the title; champions of his day, concerned about their ability to duck his punches, ducked him instead. They turned him into a perennial contender. But Benton does not care, not anymore, because he made up for it as a trainer, a career that represents one of the greatest ironies in boxing. Benton, who could not win a title inside the ring, has won ten outside, in the corner. He trained ten world champions, including heavyweight king Evander

filled with fine ladies. The trainer owned more suits and shoes than he could ever wear, and he knew it, but he kept buying more and more because he remembered "going without" as a kid in the ghettos of north Philadelphia. When Holyfield knocked out James "Buster" Douglas on October 25, 1990, the trainer earned $1 million for the fight, and he was so proud that he kept the check in his wallet for months. "Who would believe that I'd ever make that kind of money?" he asked, shaking his head. "Who would believe it?"

Benton was a hard-nosed kid, and he proved it in the neighborhood gym, developing the style that he would pass on to his fighters. He stayed close to his opponents, moving from side to side, smothering punches with punches of his own. It was not flashy, but it was effective, a style that earned him the nickname "the Professor." "I got to see a lot of great fighters in that gym," he recalled. "Ray Robinson used to come, and people would be lined up on the street, waiting to get in and see him."

A popular boxer in Philadelphia, Benton fought until the summer of 1970, when a gunshot wound ended his ring career—and almost his life. He was standing on a street corner in north Philadelphia, enjoying the night with some buddies, when he was shot in the back by a gunman who had quarreled with his brother, Henry. Police arrested a suspect who, when released on bail, was shot and killed in a gun battle only two weeks later. "I don't even like to talk about that now," said Benton, who was 37 when he was shot. "That incident is done with. But who knows how long I could have gone in boxing?"

With his boxing career over, Benton focused on training, apprenticing under the great Eddie Futch, who was working the corner for Joe Frazier, then the heavyweight champion of the world. "When I'm around anyone in boxing who knows what he's doing, I keep my eyes and ears open," Benton said. "That's what

I did with Eddie. He knew his business. He knew how to handle his fighters. He was a good teacher and a good gentleman, and I learned a lot from him."

A great chef as well as a great trainer, Benton loved to cook for his fighters. One day, while preparing a catfish dinner in the kitchen, he peered into the living room, where his fighters were watching old fight tapes. Benton stopped to watch the grainy black-and-white image on the screen, and he was impressed by one of the fighters, who had just scored a vicious knockout. "Hey, that guy's pretty good," Benton said, still holding onto the frying pan. "Who is it?" It was Benton, proving that great trainers are also great judges of talent.

## Emanuel Steward

It was a hot, humid night in Wooster, Massachusetts, the site of the 1992 Olympic boxing trials, and Emanuel Steward walked up to the hotel bar, where the sportswriters were downing beers and shots of whiskey. "I'll have a chardonnay," Steward said softly. So there you have it. In a world of beer and whiskey, a rough world in which gentility is measured by how many of your verbs start with the letter F, Steward is a chardonnay kind of guy. Ah, but is he really? Sure,

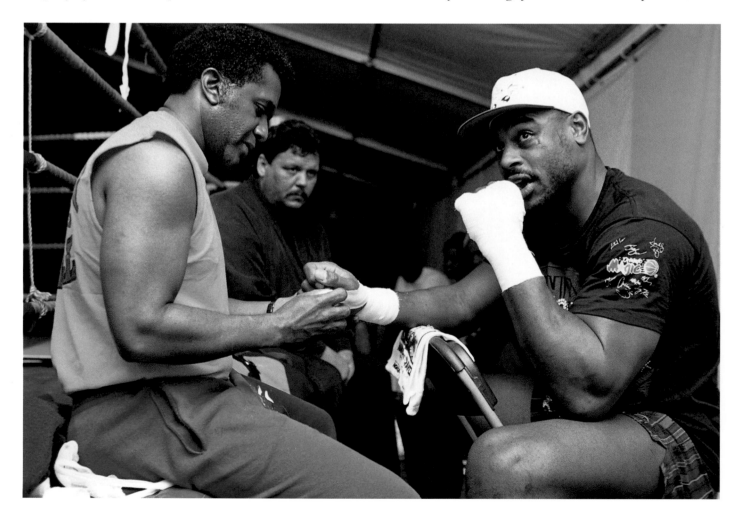

Steward, an impeccable dresser, wears dapper suits with white handkerchiefs neatly tucked in the coat pockets, and sure, he drinks, uh, char-do-nnay. But that is outside the arena. Inside the arena, in the corner, he is one of the toughest men in boxing. He once threatened to walk out on a fighter in the middle of a fight because he felt the man was not trying hard enough. "I want this more than you do," Steward screamed at him.

Steward, the leader of the legendary Kronk Gym in Detroit, saves his gentility for outside the ring. Born on July 7, 1944, in Welch, West Virginia, Steward was 8 years old when he received the greatest Christmas present of his life—boxing gloves. He became fascinated with the basic goal of the sport—to hit and not get hit—and when the family moved to Detroit, he became a national Golden Gloves champion. Then he got a job as the boxing coach for the Kronk Recreation Center. "I love fighters who fight," he said. He advocates a kamikaze style of boxing, a style that has proved remarkably successful. Steward trained the legendary Thomas "the Hit Man" Hearns, the greatest fighter to emerge from that gladiator school in Detroit. Hearns, born in 1958, is still fighting, but he is not the only superb fighter Steward has trained during his career. He has also trained world champions such as Mike McCallum, Dennis Andries, Milt McCrory, Hilmer Kenty, Jimmy Paul, Duane Thomas, Michael Moorer, and John David Jackson—most of them succeeding with the aggressive style that their trainer preaches.

If Hearns is "the Hit Man," then Steward has become the hired gun. He is the "Mr. Fix-it" of boxing, a guy who is called upon to train already successful fighters. Steward turns gyms into repair shops, using tools that he keeps in his head—knowledge and common sense—and the fighters appreciate it. He tinkers with a boxing style, making a suggestion here and there, and then he moves on to his next subject, his next world champion. He is a modern-day paladin—have gloves, will travel. The trainer has worked with Evander Holyfield, Julio Cesar Chavez, and Oscar De

OPPOSITE: Seen here on September 24, 1994, trainer Emanuel Steward tapes the hands of Lennox Lewis before a fight against Oliver McCall. Steward consistently lives up to his name, in this case guiding Lewis to victory with his wise stewardship. RIGHT: Tex Rickard (seated, center) was the legendary promoter who brought P.T. Barnum–style showmanship to the art of drawing a fight crowd. Rickard promoted many of the fights featuring Jack Dempsey (seated, left), including the first bout in history to draw a million-dollar gate.

La Hoya, each time successfully. "Oscar De La Hoya is already a diamond," Steward said before joining the fighter briefly in 1997. "I just want to polish it."

## The Promoters

### Tex Rickard

A dapper man in a bow tie and straw hat, George Lewis "Tex" Rickard looked like a refugee from a Broadway musical, his cane more of a prop than a walking aid. But he was no fancy pants—not Tex Rickard. No, he was a man who stubbornly, if elegantly, refused to believe in the calendar. After all, this was the 1900s, but he had one foot in the nineteenth century, and he refused to drag it across the time line. Boxing

loved him for it, because it was this time warp that gave the man his charm, his toughness, his ability to turn lackluster bouts into matches that electrified the world. Rickard could have sold hot chocolate in the Mojave Desert, and the sportswriters loved him for it. They called him "the greatest sports promoter" on the planet.

Rickard worked at a gambling house in the boomtown of Goldfield, Nevada, and he was a man whose job fit his personality perfectly. He mingled among his people—the cowboys, the prospectors, the daredevils who would do anything for a buck—and tried to lure them into the house, where the gambling tables and the roulette wheels would do the rest. Rickard was a great host, and the qualities that made him a great host—charm, vision, resourcefulness—would also make him a great promoter.

When his business partners wanted to promote a fight in Goldfield, they picked the right man for the job—Rickard. He staged the lightweight title fight between Joe Gans and Battling Nelson on September 3, 1906, and he proved as entertaining as the fighters themselves. Gans won the fight in 42 rounds, but what Rickard did will last longer. It will last forever, because it became part of history, bringing sports promotions into the twentieth century—a pretty ironic situation for a former gold prospector who loved the rough-and-tumble life of the past. "A showman, that was Tex Rickard," sportswriter Hype Igoe wrote.

Rickard proved it with the Gans-Nelson bout by drawing nationwide publicity when he displayed the $30,000 purse in tall stacks of freshly minted $20 gold pieces. The fight attracted eight thousand fans, and it drew what was then the richest gate in boxing history—$90,000. Not bad for a sport whose contestants once fought on barges to escape the authorities. Yes, no doubt about it, Rickard, the nineteenth-century man, was yanking the sport into the twentieth century.

The promoter also staged the heavyweight title fight between Jack Johnson and Jim Jeffries, "the Great White Hope," in Reno, Nevada—the most significant bout since the Marquess of Queensberry rules. Johnson, who knocked Jeffries out in the 15th round, earned what was the biggest purse in boxing history, $120,000, while Jeffries, a farmer who had come out of retirement, earned $90,000—staggering amounts for a sport that staged, in the beginning, human cockfights.

Rickard did not stop there; he took boxing on a ride that would lead to the multimillion-dollar bouts common today. He promoted the Jack Dempsey–Georges Carpentier heavyweight title bout on July 2, 1921, in Jersey City, New Jersey—the first million-dollar gate in boxing history at $1,789,238. Dempsey clubbed the challenger in the 4th round, a ridiculously easy match, but nobody cared; the spectacle seemed more important than the competition itself. "It will be many, many years...before another Tex Rickard will be seen in action," Igoe wrote.

The Dempsey-Charpentier fight was so huge that *The New York Times* devoted most of its issue, not just the sports section, to coverage of the spectacle on July 3, 1921. "One thing is sure," Irvin S. Cobb reported. "Today, Boyle's Thirty Acres has given to Tex Rickard a richer harvest than any like area of this world's surface has ever yielded."

## Don King

There he is, his hair defying gravity, his sentences defying syntax—the greatest promoter in the world, according to a gargantuan, if not objective, source: himself. Don King will promote his sport tirelessly, hyping a fight until his magnificent voice sags to a whisper, his trademark cackle ("Heh, heh, heh") getting fainter and fainter. And a promoter without a voice is like a stripper without a tabletop.

But if there is one thing that King likes to promote more than his sport, it is himself. The man is his own press agent, each outburst representing another release from the publicity machine. He makes a pronouncement and takes an almost childlike joy in his words, laughing as if he were a member of the audience, as enthralled as everybody else—heh, heh, heh—at his remarks, some of which are almost impossible to decipher. His malapropisms make Archie Bunker look like an English professor. Consider these statements:

He once referred to his lawyer as his "banister."

He once said he had a "plutonic" relationship with Ruth Roper, the former mother-in-law of Mike Tyson.

He once said Tyson is like "Manyshnikov."

He once referred to basketball player Sam Bowie as a hero of the Alamo.

And then there is the hair. King says it is an act of God. One day, it was flat; the next day, it was rising toward the heavens, like plants searching for the sunlight. King may be outrageous, but regardless of what people think of him—and he has more detractors than anybody in the fight game—they would have to admit one thing: the man is charming. It is a strange charm, perhaps, the kind a snake oil salesman might employ, but it is a charm nonetheless. "It transcends earthly bounds," King once said.

Don King points a finger at fellow promoter Butch Lewis, standing on the opposite side of real estate tycoon (and casino owner) Donald Trump.

Well, maybe not. But King does transcend boxing. Everybody knows the promoter—everybody, and that includes people who do not know a right cross from a right turn on red after stop. And nothing pleases him more. He is so self-absorbed that after one fight, gripped by an attack of self-pity, he spent more than an hour threatening to resign from the fight game. The poor pugs who were eager to speak at the postfight press conference never got the chance. King was on a roll. The next morning, he forgot what he had said, and the retirement party was off.

And why should he retire, his supporters would ask. He is the most successful promoter in boxing history, a man whose grip on the sport—and hold on the public—has grown since he began staging fights in the Muhammad Ali era. He has promoted some of the greatest fights in history, fights that will be discussed in bars and taverns for as long as men make fists for a living, such as the "Thrilla in Manilla," the "Rumble in the Jungle," and the two fights between Evander Holyfield and Mike Tyson, including the infamous ear-biting incident.

A former numbers runner who spent four years in prison for manslaughter, King began to dominate the boxing scene in 1974, and has promoted more than three hundred world title fights since then. But it has not been easy. The list of fighters who have sued him, usually citing fraud and breach of contract, reads like a who's who: Larry Holmes, Tim Witherspoon, Mike Tyson, Julio Cesar Chavez. Once, trying to make peace with Chavez, King flew to Culiacan, Mexico, the home of the great former champion, where the promoter said he hopped on a burro and yelled to the townspeople, "Donde es Julio? Donde es Julio?"

The FBI has investigated King since the 1980s, usually for the alleged offenses cited by his fighters, but they have never been able to nail him—evidence, he likes to say, of what a great country America is. "If this were Russia," he once said, "I'd be a black ice cube in Siberia." The latest acquittal came in 1998, this one on charges of insurance fraud involving a policy from Lloyd's of London. It was, for King, another example of a wonderful judicial system at work, and he repaid some important members of that system after the trial—the jury that acquitted him. He took them to the Bahamas, all at his own expense—an outrageous show of thanks that he has extended before, to other jurors, at other trials, on other charges. "Only in America," King likes to crow.

When James "Buster" Douglas upset Tyson (then promoted by King) on February 11, 1990, the promoter screamed about an alleged long count that kept his fighter from hanging on to his title. This controversy,

regarded as a transparent ploy by most boxing observers, led two U.S. representatives to sponsor bills to create a federal boxing commission. "Don, you've done some good things for boxing," Representative Bill Richard (D-N.M.) told King on *Crossfire*, a cable program. "But you're part of the problem. You have too much power."

"How can you say that?" King responded. "You're a congressman. How can you say that? I work very hard, and I do so in the American way. I'm trying to emulate and imitate what success means in America, and I'm condemned for it. Why? Why?"

Whether you love him or hate him—and most boxing fans fall in one category or the other—King is a born debater, malapropisms and all.

## Bob Arum

If promoters were wallflowers, they would not be able to stage a fight between Jimmy and Rocko on the corner of South and Broad in South Philadelphia, much

less a "Thrilla in Manilla" or a "Rumble in the Jungle." But shyness is for the cut men, the guys who carry the spit buckets, not for the promoters. And yet, next to Don King, Bob Arum looks like a mute. But do not be deceived. Arum is one of the most successful promoters in boxing history, and he can talk with the best of them, even if, unlike King, he does not speak as if he has a microphone lodged in his throat. Remember, it was Arum who, caught in an inconsistency, once said, "Yesterday, I was lying. Today, I'm telling the truth."

The promoter is one of the most erudite men in the fight game—and one of the shrewdest. A lawyer who was hired by Robert Kennedy, then the attorney general in the administration of his brother, Arum helped the government win landmark decisions against corporate giants such as Con Edison, Citibank, and Standard Oil. Then, in 1962, he fought to secure the proceeds from the Sonny Liston–Floyd Patterson heavyweight title fight, which were rumored to be heading out of the country. It was his introduction to the world of boxing, a world that fascinated him. "My essential strength as a promoter is that I'm a good administrator," Arum said.

While Don King has virtually monopolized the heavyweight division since the 1970s, Bob Arum has retreated to the lighter weights, promoting some of the biggest fights in history, including the middleweight title fight between "Marvelous" Marvin Hagler and Sugar Ray Leonard on April 6, 1987. He called it the "Fight of the Century"—and the anticipation, if not the competition itself, warranted a tag that had been used countless times before. How many fights of the century can there be? Quite a few, apparently.

The promoter, trying to hype the significance of the bout, arranged for a round table among the great middleweight champions of the past—Jake LaMotta, Rocky Graziano, Carmen Basilio, Joey Giardello, Paul Pender, and Vito Antuofermo. They met at a steak house in Manhattan, some of them threatening to pound the raw meat dangling from the ceiling, and they predicted the outcome of the bout. Most of them picked Hagler, and Graziano, when asked for the strategy he would pursue against Leonard, replied, "I'd try

to take his eyes out." Leonard, his eyes intact, upset Hagler.

Arum also tapped a market that the other promoters failed to recognize—the Latino market. Oh, King promoted Chavez for years, but he usually relegated him to undercards on Mike Tyson fights, turning a marquee performer into a warm-up act. Arum was different. He treated Oscar De La Hoya, the latest Latino sensation, like "the Golden Boy," the nickname he had earned when he became the only U.S. boxer to win a gold medal in the 1992 Olympics.

De La Hoya has become a huge star, not just as an attraction on cable TV but also at the grassroots level, in the towns where he fights, the most wondrous example being El Paso, Texas. "The Golden Boy" fought there on June 13, 1998, and the fans followed him everywhere, from the airport to the hotel to the gym—thousands of shrieking females, one of whom tossed her bra at the fighter after his plane landed at the airport. De La Hoya autographed the undergarment, which will probably never get close to a washing machine again. It was phenomenal. "This is unprecedented," said Nigel Collins, the editor of *Ring Magazine*. "The fighter as teen idol." De La Hoya fought Patrick Charpentier, a pug who might have drawn five thousand fans, six thousand tops, in a venue like Las Vegas. But El Paso was not Las Vegas; the fight attracted 45,368 fans, one of the largest crowds to witness a fight in this country since September 15, 1978, when Muhammad Ali fought Leon Spinks before 63,350 fans in the New Orleans Superdome. "The fans [at my fight] were the best I've ever seen in my career," De La Hoya said.

## The Duva Family

It was like a mom-and-pop grocery store—without the street corner. No, their street corner was the world. They promoted fights from New York to Paris, from Wales to Germany, and they did it as a family. The patriarch was Lou Duva, born in 1921, a former trucker and bail bondsman who once compared himself to Fred Flintstone. Fred Flintstone? Duva made the caveman seem shy and retiring. Duva once took a pop at junior welterweight Roger Mayweather, who had just defeated one of his fighters, Vinny Pazienza. Duva, upset about what he took to be an apparent foul, stormed into the ring after the fight, actually taking a shot at the former champion, who promptly fired back. For his troubles, Duva ended up with a bloody nose—certainly not the first time for this man who got his start in amateur boxing through barroom smokers in Paterson, New Jersey.

In 1984, the family hit the big time, acquiring four world champions—Johnny Bumphus, Rocky Lockridge, Livingstone Bramble, and Mike McCallum. But it would not stop there; with the help of Shelly Finkel, a big-time entertainment manager, the family signed five gold medal winners from the 1984 Olympics: Evander Holyfield, Pernell "Sweetpea" Whitaker, Mark Breland,

If Duva was loud and brash, it was just what the family operation needed—a spark of emotion and determination. The family started out small, with Lou, his son Dan, and his daughter-in-law Kathy promoting boxing events at Ice World in Totowa, New Jersey. It was not exactly Madison Square Garden, but their passion made up for the crummy digs. Lou trained the fighters, Kathy handled the publicity, and Dan, a graduate of Seton Hall Law School, handled the nuts and bolts of the promotion. "Those were good days," Lou said.

Meldrick Taylor, and Tyrell Biggs, with Biggs the only one who didn't win a world title. "I think everyone should fight—everyone," said Lou, who boasted a pro record of 15-7. "Everyone should step into the ring to see what it's like."

Dan died of a brain tumor in 1996, and his younger brother, Dino, has assumed the promotional duties with the same grace and dignity.

ABOVE: Teddy Atlas (left) and Lou Duva (background) counsel heavyweight Michael Moorer.

# Self-Management: the Saga of "Gypsy" Joe

Not all fighters have had the benefit of a good manager or trainer—some have had to do it all for themselves. More than any other boxer in history, Gypsy Joe Harris embodied the traits of a manager, trainer, and promoter. He promoted himself tirelessly, and if he had not been a wily, cunning manager of his own career, he would not have had a career at all. As for training, Harris, who was blind in one eye since childhood, had to devise his own strategy in fight after fight. In the end, unfortunately, Harris did not have the career his skills might have suggested, but his life inside and outside the ring was a compelling one.

Harris, nicknamed "Gypsy" because of his fancy dress and carefree attitude (he was known to change outfits three or four times a day), loved the crowds—in and out of the arena. He worked as a bartender during his fighting days—not because he needed the money, but because he liked the warmth of the fans who frequented the place. They would line up at the bar, and he would regale them with tales of his exploits in the ring, as well as his ambitions: "Be champ of the world. Make a lot of money. That was the dream."

For Harris, the most glorious moment came on March 31, 1967, in Madison Square Garden, when he took a unanimous 10-round decision over welterweight champion Curtis Cokes. More than five hundred Philadelphia fans made the trip to see their hero, and they returned hailing him as the uncrowned champion in the wake of his masterful triumph.

After Cokes, Harris fought eight more times, losing only once, a decision to former champion Emile Griffith on August 6, 1968, in Philadelphia, where a crowd of 13,875 witnessed the fight. He earned the biggest payday of his career—$12,500—for that bout, but it was to be his last.

On the morning of October 11, 1968, Harris was taking a prefight physical for his bout against Manny Gonzalez at the Arena in Philadelphia. Dr. Wilbur H. Strickland, noticing an inflammation of the right eye, took the fighter to University Hospital for a more thorough checkup. It was there that Dr. Harold G. Scheie determined that Harris was blind in one eye.

"My camp knew I was blind," Harris said in a later interview. Alas, the key figures in that camp—promoter Herman Taylor, manager Yank Durham, and trainer Willie Reddish—had since died, so there was no way to confirm or dispute the contention that they knew about the bad eye from the beginning.

In an even more alarming allegation, however, Harris claimed afterward that the athletic commission knew about his bad eye and let him continue fighting because he was such a popular attraction in Philadelphia.

"I told the press that I had been memorizing the eye chart all those years, but I was just trying to protect the commission," Harris said. "They knew about my eye from the beginning. Let me ask you a question. How can a man have a license to examine a person and not realize I was blind?... I turned professional in '65, and they stopped me in '68. Were the doctors sleeping from '65 to '68? Did they just find out?"

In 1972, Harris filed an appeal to have his license reinstated. During a public hearing, Strickland, who died in 1987, acknowledged that the commission realized as early as 1966 that Harris suffered from "defective vision"—but not total blindness—in his right eye. As Harris continued fighting, the doctor said, the eye became more of a concern to the commission, until the organization finally barred him from the ring.

"How much longer would you fight if you got your license?" Zach Clayton, then head of the commission, asked Harris.

"Two or three years," Harris said.

"And what would you do then?"

"Be rich."

Harris lost his appeal.

One of the most popular boxers ever to fight in Philadelphia, Harris had built up a record of 24-1 before the commission "discovered" that he was blind in his right eye. He lost the use of that eye when he was eleven years old, but turned the disability into an asset. In fact, Harris boasted the most creative boxing style since Sugar Ray Robinson, dipping, bending, and twisting to keep his his good eye—his left—on his opponent.

Ironically, the handicap that made him great led to the end of his career, the end of his dream. After his boxing license was taken away, the former No. 1 contender in the world—a man whose fortitude and confidence had given him the strength to overcome so many obstacles in his life—resorted to drugs and liquor. He was trying to kill himself, and when the heroin and whiskey failed to do the trick, he tried something else. One night in 1979, he walked across the Ben Franklin Bridge, intent on diving into the river and drowning himself.

"When your mind is so upset, you're not thinking right, and you'll go and do anything," he recalled. "I was up on that bridge. I told myself I was going to jump off. But then, I thought, 'Hey, I can swim.' I got a little medal for swimming at the recreation center when I was a kid. It seemed kind of funny later. Here I was. I wanted to drown myself, and I could swim."

When his license was revoked, Harris found a job as a street cleaner, then as a construction worker, then as a.... He had forgotten all the jobs he held, but there was one thing he never forgot—the misery he experienced in all of them. Harris was a fighter, and when they took away his right to dance and batter a man in front of a crowd, he lost his heart.

After years of being down and out, Harris suffered three cardiac arrests in 1988—the result, he was certain, of all the time he had spent abusing his body with drugs and alcohol. When it became clear that the on-again, off-again hospitalization wasn't doing the trick, Harris finally kicked the habit on his own. "I said, 'The hell with it.' I went off of it, and I had to stay in the bathroom for days. After three or four days, I didn't need drugs no more. I was cured. I was weak, but I didn't have the urge anymore."

Following his battles with heart disease and addiction, both perhaps the aftereffects of a dream deferred, Harris died on March 6, 1990. His life and career were both a testament to how much a man can accomplish on his own as well as a warning about the fragility of the boxing life.

# GREAT FIGHTS  4

It was not a fight. It was a slaughter, a massacre. Any audience, save a prize-fighting one,
would have exhausted its emotions in that first minute.
—Jack London, *The Mexican*

**G**reat boxing matches are massive relocation projects. They bring street fights indoors, creating a sense of excitement—and dread—unlike any other sporting event in the world. They provide controlled mayhem—fury tempered by guile and artistry. And fans remember the bouts long after the fighters have taken off their gloves. Who remembers Super Bowl VI? Or the 1976 NBA finals? Or the 1991 World Series? But a fight, ah, a fight will remain in your memory banks forever, almost as if your mind were a scrapbook. And your memory becomes sharper, more vivid, as the years go on; it recalls details that you may have missed the first time around. Why are fights so exciting? It is the artistry and athleticism, yes, but more than that, it is the sense of danger. The combinations that thrill you one minute can fill you with a sense of dread the next, when the poor pug is unconscious, stretched out on the canvas. "I'm in the hurt business," the great Sugar Ray Robinson once said. Right or wrong, it is that brutality which attracts us to the sport, even though part of us may be disgusted by the ugly spectacle.

If we accept that the attraction to a boxing match is an uneasy combination of the baser and nobler sides of human nature, what is it that makes a particular fight great? Some slugfests go the full 15 rounds and elicit little more than a groan of relief from a bored stadium crowd, while some last only into the first few rounds and are remembered forever. Well, if the initial attraction is a dichotomy, the elements of history's great fights reflect the same dual nature: some achieve legendary status because they showcase incredible feats of bravery and endurance, while others stick in our minds because of their ferocity and violence. For instance, though the contest happened in 1919, no one who is a fan of boxing history will forget the fight between Jack Dempsey and Jess Willard; the spectacular and surprising violence Dempsey unleashed on Willard left the larger man with a shattered face and only lasted 3 rounds. Meanwhile, Willie Pep's remarkable comeback victory over Sandy Saddler in 1949 for the featherweight title was a tribute to man's ability to overcome tragedy (Pep had been in a life-threatening plane crash less than two years earlier), face great odds, and still triumph.

Above: In one of the most sensational bouts of the era, Roberto Duran and Sugar Ray Leonard fight for their lives during their June 20, 1980, middleweight title bout in Montreal. Opposite: Playing David to Jess Willard's Goliath on July 4, 1919, challenger Jack Dempsey (left) assesses his much larger opponent across the ring. The far quicker Dempsey didn't take long to figure out how to take down the giant; after 3 rounds of terrible abuse, a broken and battered Jess Willard could not go on.

### Jack Dempsey vs. Jess Willard
### July 4, 1919

They called it "pugilistic murder," a fight so brutal that the referee could have doubled as a coroner. Jack Dempsey, thirteen years younger and almost 70 pounds (32kg) lighter than the heavyweight champion, looked like a toddler challenging the neighborhood bully. He

a man so massive? Jess Willard then threw his first punch of the fight, a left that missed. Dempsey countered the punch with a hailstorm of blows, dropping the champion seven times—yes, seven times—in the 1st round. The challenger stood over the fallen fighter each time, ready to pound him again and again.

The fight lasted 3 rounds, with Willard dazed and bloodied on his stool, a man who had entered the ring

ABOVE: Dempsey punches Willard into a corner during their landmark bout on July 4, 1919, while the U.S. flag flaps in the breeze.

seemed lost and timid in the opening moments of the fight as he cautiously circled his opponent for about a minute. Could this be "the Manassa Mauler," the man who had scored five consecutive 1st-round knockouts? But there was a good reason for this strategy. Dempsey was not timid so much as confused. How could he beat

with a confidence that deserted him with the first left hook to the jaw. The former champion sat in the corner, his eyes vacant; he was as defenseless on the stool as he had been in the ring. Yes, he was a huge man, but Dempsey had countered size with fury, leading sportswriters to coin the term "killer instinct."

They called it the "Massacre at Toledo," and Willard claimed that his opponent had "loaded" his gloves by treating his hand tape with a talcum substance that turned hard as concrete when wet. Perhaps. But Dempsey insisted that his fists did all the damage, enough damage to keep a hospital emergency room busy for weeks—a broken jaw, a split cheekbone, a busted nose, a battered ear, and six broken teeth. Willard never regained proper hearing in his left ear.

## Joe Louis vs. Billy Conn
## June 18, 1941

Pity the man on the verge of accomplishing the impossible. Why? Because he begins to savor the view from the mountaintop before he has even reached it. He gets cocky and arrogant, and he starts to make the tiny mistakes that great opponents turn into huge mistakes. Billy Conn knew the feeling.

Conn, the light heavyweight champion of the world, met Joe Louis, the heavyweight king, at the Polo Grounds in New York. It was an act of audacity just to face Louis, let alone think you could beat him. But Conn thought he could, even though the heavyweight champion outweighed him by about 30 pounds (14kg). "I beat the main fellows, the contenders, so I figured we'll try Joe Louis, he's just another guy," Conn said. "You don't fight guys like Joe Louis unless you beat all those guys that really knew how to fight, and then you learn how to fight. You're not just some mug coming in off the street corner to fight Joe Louis, because he'd knock you through the middle of next week."

Armed with confidence and ring savvy, Conn outboxed the heavyweight champion through the middle rounds, taking control of the match with his superior

ABOVE: Light heavyweight Billy Conn was on top of this June 18, 1941, fight against heavyweight Joe Louis, when he became overconfident and tried to knock out the Brown Bomber in the 13th round. It was an ill-advised change in strategy and Louis made the quicker, more agile challenger pay for the mistake with this crushing left hook that sent Conn to the mat for good.

speed. The light heavyweight king boxed brilliantly, executing a game plan that was an amazing combination of daring and caution. He charged inside to land one, two, three, four blows in a row before darting back outside, almost as if he were both participant and spectator, firing punches one second, admiring his handiwork the next. Conn was in a rhythm, a rhythm he had never experienced before, not against an opponent as talented and menacing as Louis, and he loved it. He stunned the heavyweight champion with a left hook to the jaw in the 12th round, but it was a curious blow, a blow that hurt Conn much more than it did Louis, because it turned a confident man into an overconfident man. "I hurt him in the 12th round, so I figured I'll try and knock him out," Conn said. "I made a mistake. He was waiting for me. He'd have never hit me in the ass if I didn't make a mistake and try to knock him out."

Conn, ahead on two of the three scorecards, rejected the advice of his corner, which was to box cautiously so that he could preserve the win that seemed all but certain. He went for the knockout in the 13th round, charging inside without retreating back outside, as he had done in the earlier rounds, when he built up his lead. Then Louis smashed him with a left hook to the jaw, and just like that, the fight was over. "They told me to stay away from him, that I was beating him all the way," Conn said. "But when I hurt him in the 12th round, he started to hold on. I said, 'I'm going to knock this son of a bitch out. Don't worry about it.'"

So he went out for the 13th round, and he told Louis, "Well, Joe, you're in for a tough fight tonight." Louis flattened him a few seconds later, standing over his opponent to get in the final words. "You're right," Louis said.

Later, Conn found humor in his missed opportunity. "I told my corner, 'Don't worry about it. I'm going to knock him out.' Don't worry about it? And then I made one mistake!"

## Muhammad Ali vs. Joe Frazier
## March 8, 1971

Forget about Muhammad Ali and Joe Frazier as individuals. They were great fighters, two of the best heavyweights who ever lived, but together, ah, together they reached heights that went beyond greatness. What is the next elevator stop after greatness? It may be too mind-numbing to comprehend, but whatever it is, these two men reached it.

Ali and Frazier were opposites—one tall and pretty, the other short and squat—but the odd couple gave fight fans the most legendary trilogy in boxing history, 123 minutes of fury and elegance, guile and grace, comedy and drama. They also gave us 123 minutes of themselves. Who could have asked for more?

In an age when heavyweights wage their fiercest battles at the negotiating table, demanding more money for less risk, it is worth remembering that Ali and Frazier earned every penny they made. They fought each other three times, but their first battle, on March 8, 1971, in Madison Square Garden, was the best—better than their second meeting, which Ali won by decision on January 28, 1974. The first was even better than their third and final struggle, the fabled "Thrilla in Manilla," won by Ali with a dramatic 14th-round technical knockout on October 1, 1975. "They left a little bit of themselves in the ring," said Eddie Futch, the legendary trainer who worked the corner for Frazier, of the first fight. "They hit their peak that night, and that's saying something."

Ali and Frazier were undefeated, each with a legitimate claim to the heavyweight crown—Frazier because he held the official title, Ali because he lost his outside the ring, where boxing organizations stripped him of his belt for his refusal to be inducted into the armed services. "It was the greatest boxing event I've ever covered," said Ed Schuyler, Jr., the great boxing writer who has covered more than three hundred world title fights for the Associated Press.

The bout attracted 20,455 fans to the Garden, most of them members of the "beautiful people" set. Frank Sinatra took pictures for *Life* magazine, and Burt Lancaster provided the commentary for the closed-circuit telecast. It was like an issue of *People* come to life. "It was packed with celebrities," Schuyler said. "But it was the only fight I've ever witnessed where the celebrities went to see, not to be seen. The stars were the two guys in the ring....By the 9th round, everybody in the arena was standing up."

OPPOSITE: The first installment of what is perhaps the most fabled trilogy of heavyweight match-ups was aired on March 8, 1971, when Muhammad Ali battled Joe Frazier for the world title.

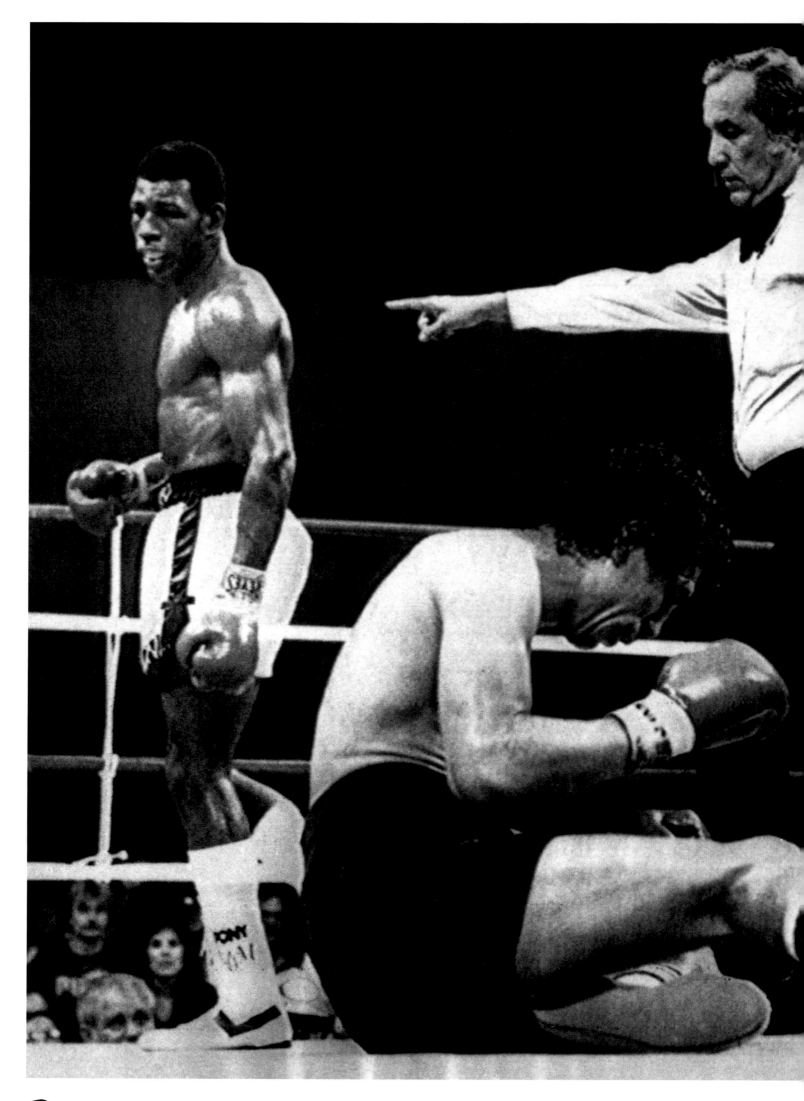

Ali danced and preened early in the fight, going toe-to-toe in the later rounds when his stamina began to fade. It faded at a bad time, because the longer the fight went on, the fresher the champion seemed. Frazier, stalking his opponent from the start, dropped Ali in the 15th and final round—perhaps the most famous knockdown in boxing history. "I was surprised that Ali got up so quickly," said Arthur Mercante, who refereed the fight. "I had only reached the count of 2. I had never seen anyone recover from a punch like that. It was a tremendous, thunderous left hook. Floyd Patterson hit Ingemar Johannson with a similar shot, but Johannson stayed on the canvas for a long, long time."

Ali almost went down earlier, in the 11th round, but just as his legs were about to cave in, his magnificent heart kept him up. "Ali was out on his feet, and Joe could have knocked him out in that round," Futch said. "But Ali was smart. He started clowning, and he made Joe think he was playing possum. But he wasn't. He was really hurt."

When it was all over, 15 brutal rounds after it started, boxing had an undisputed heavyweight champion. Frazier captured a unanimous decision, and Ali had an easy explanation—"I got hit," he said. The winner flashed a grotesque smile, a stream of blood pouring from a mouth that had been pounded mercilessly for forty-five minutes. "It was a great fight and an unbelievable spectacle, just unbelievable," boxing historian Bert Sugar said. "I haven't seen that kind of passion in the ring since."

## Matthew Saad Muhammad vs. Yaqui Lopez
## July 13, 1980

If you look at most retired fighters, you will see their records on their faces—the wins and losses stamped on the lumpy ears, the busted noses, the scar tissue that covers their faces like a thick crust. Matthew Saad Muhammad, the former light heavyweight champion, is different. His face is smooth and unmarked, as if he had spent all those years selling insurance, not taking punches. But he did take punches, lots of them, and his face should be designated as one of the wonders of the world because it should be covered with scars—especially when you consider his battle with Yaqui Lopez

LEFT: Light heavyweight champion Matthew Saad Muhammad overcame an early beating and was able to stop challenger Yaqui Lopez in the 14th round of their title bout on June 13, 1980.

on July 13, 1980, at the Playboy Club in McAfee, New Jersey.

Both men took enough punches to deck a gym full of fighters, but Saad Muhammad took more blows early, and Lopez looked like a certain winner. The champion seemed spent by the 5th round; he looked so tired that he resembled one of those marathon dancers, his feet dragging across the floor as he draped himself across his partner, Lopez, who proved to be a partner from hell. The challenger took some shots, too, but he seemed to deliver five for every one he took, and the outcome seemed inevitable to the TV announcers, who thought Saad Muhammad would lose by knockout. "Man, I get a headache every time I see that fight," the champion said years later.

Saad Muhammad took twenty unanswered blows in the 8th round, but the referee did not halt the bout, and the champion recovered, crossing that threshold that seems to separate gifted fighters from oblivion: once they survive the most brutal combinations of their opponents, they are fine; they can take anything from that moment on, and Saad Muhammad did just that. He absorbed the blows and delivered some of his own, coming back so furiously that he floored his opponent four times in the 14th and final round. "I hit him good, but he would not go down," Lopez said. "That's why he's champion."

To this day, the former champion is amazed that he took those shots. "I'm a warrior, and a warrior will not stay down unless he's unconscious," Saad Muhammad said. "But, ooh, how did I take those punches?"

## Aaron Pryor vs. Alexis Arguello
## November 12, 1982

Alexis Arguello was a smooth, elegant boxer, a man who could inflict more damage with a single punch than most fighters could with dozens of combinations. He was tall and thin, a physique that often led opponents to underestimate him, as did Kevin Rooney, who would go on to train Mike Tyson for five turbulent years in the 1980s. Rooney met Arguello on July 31, 1982, in Atlantic City, and when he spotted his opponent at the

RIGHT: In one of the most exciting boxing contests of the 1980s, Alexis Arguello (right) took on junior welterweight champ Aaron Pryor in a valiant attempt to become the first man to hold titles in four weight classes. Despite a tremendous effort, Arguello was finally knocked out by his equally skilled opponent in the 14th round.

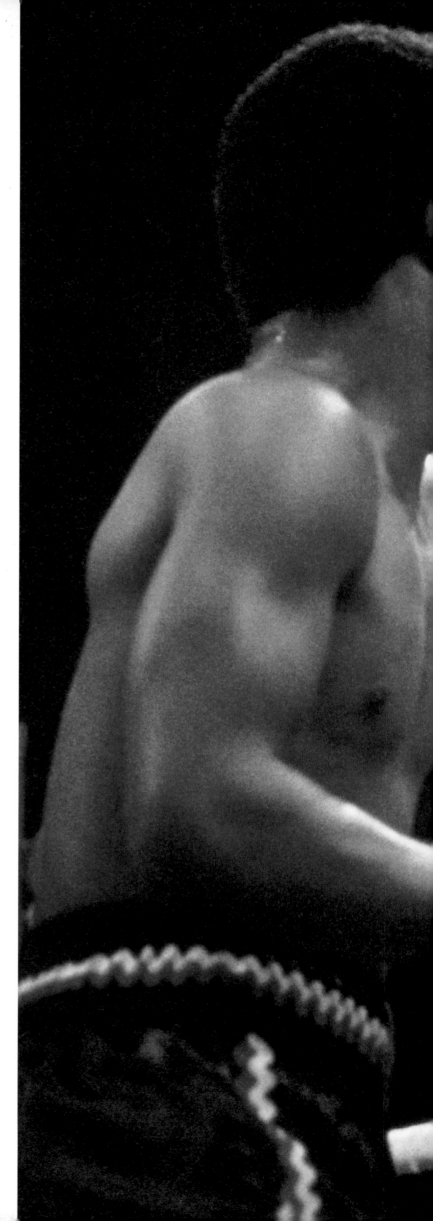

weigh-in, he thought to himself, "This guy's too skinny. I can lick him." The skinny pushover knocked him out in the 2nd round. Rooney was so dazed that a few hours later, he told his wife he had to get ready for the fight that had ended so quickly.

As ambitious as he was efficient, Arguello was attempting to become the first man in history to win world titles in four weight classes. There was only one problem. He was facing Aaron Pryor, the junior welterweight champion, a man who was equally ambitious—and equally talented. He was also the most intimidating man in boxing. Whenever he stepped into the ring, Pryor would point his right arm at his opponent, holding it as if he were staring through the sights of a shotgun. Fans called him "the Hawk."

They met before 23,800 fans at the Orange Bowl in Miami—a crowd that witnessed perhaps the greatest fight of the 1980s. Pryor won the early rounds, throwing punches from all angles, a whirlwind of combinations that seemed impossible to defend against. The champion boxed in the middle rounds, and the challenger began to rally, landing right hands that would have crushed most fighters—most fighters, but not Pryor. Arguello landed an amazing flurry in the 13th round—punch after punch after punch—but he did

more damage to himself than to his opponent by tiring himself out with the fusillade. Pryor rallied in the 14th round, throwing the same kind of combinations that his opponent had hurled only moments earlier. Arguello did not weather them as successfully. He retreated to the ropes, taking more punishment before finally crumpling, unconscious, to the canvas.

## "Marvelous" Marvin Hagler vs. Thomas Hearns
## April 15, 1985

The fight lasted only 7 minutes and 52 seconds, but "Marvelous" Marvin Hagler and Thomas Hearns offered the world a brief history lesson—they took us back in time by showing us how men fought before the discovery of fire. This was no "sweet science." It was furious combat, raw and ugly, and it was no less compelling for its brevity. Hearns knew he had to box, but Hagler, usually a cautious fighter, stormed into the center of the ring, and there went the game plan, as useless as a spit bucket. Hagler, the undisputed middleweight champion, fought like a challenger, but he paid for his aggressiveness, suffering a cut on his forehead with only 30 seconds left in the 1st round. "I started slugging because I had to," Hearns said.

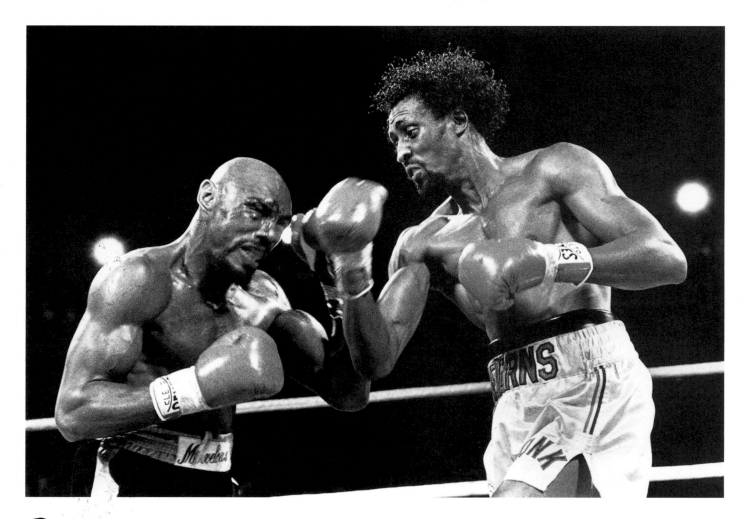

OPPOSITE: In this shot from their classic middleweight title fight, Thomas Hearns (right) crushes Marvelous Marvin Hagler with a right to the head. The passion and fury that both these men brought to this fight made it one of the most exciting ring confrontations ever. ABOVE: In the end, Hagler eventually got the better of his opponent early in the 3rd round, laying Hearns out for good with a devastating flurry of blows punctuated with a thunderous right.

Hearns kept slugging, opening another cut in the 2nd round, this one on the cheek of his opponent. How much more could Hagler take? The champion had been floored only once before, when Juan Roldan nailed him two years earlier, but Hearns was a better puncher, sharper and more accurate, and he was beating Hagler to the punch. But the champion stayed on his feet; somehow he stayed on his feet, and he dared Hearns to stay on his.

The ringside physician examined the champion before the start of the 3rd round and threatened to stop the fight on cuts. Hagler, motivated by the examination, charged at his opponent, who remained in the center of the ring, so flat-footed that he seemed to be wearing ankle weights. The champion hurt the challenger with a combination and followed up with an overhand right that dropped Hearns onto the seat of his gold silk trunks. Hearns beat the 10-count, but he looked like a sleepwalker, his eyes as glazed as a cheap doughnut. Referee Richard Steele stopped the fight and ended perhaps the greatest 3 rounds in boxing history. "Few had witnessed anything like the apocalyptic conflict," British journalist Peter Walsh wrote.

## Meldrick Taylor vs. Julio Cesar Chavez
## March 17, 1990

They were perfect opponents—one quick and flashy, the other calm and methodical—the two greatest fighters of their era, pound for pound. Meldrick Taylor was the boxer, Julio Cesar Chavez the puncher—but the labels meant nothing, not for these junior welterweights. Why? Because each fighter exhibited traits of the other: Taylor could punch and Chavez could box, each measuring his opponent with the cool intensity of a diamond appraiser. The fight promised great theater, and for once, the match lived up to the hype.

In the 1st round, Taylor seemed nervous, as if he were respectful—perhaps too respectful—of a fighter known for flattening his opponents and then shrugging his shoulders with all the remorse of a hit man. Taylor punched and retreated, darting in and out like a hummingbird, while his opponent calmly chased him. It was still early, but it was a dramatic round, with the two men setting the scene for the battle of attrition that awaited them in the later rounds.

Chavez landed a short, jolting right to the jaw in the 2nd round, a blow that sent his opponent into a Chaplinesque waddle in the middle of the ring. Taylor recovered, but the punch had dramatized the wisdom of his strategy in the 1st round. He began to bleed from the mouth.

The Philadelphian, demonstrating his dazzling hand speed for the first time in the fight, landed a solid combination in the 2nd round, but the Mexican shook his head as if the punches were affectionate pats. Taylor smiled, refusing to get frustrated. He seemed in command. "I fought the best fight I could fight," he said afterward.

In the middle rounds, Taylor abandoned his early caution by fighting on the inside in an attempt to beat his opponent at his own game. He was landing more punches, but he absorbed some in return, and the punches he took were heavier and more punishing; cuts opened in both nostrils and above both eyes. The Philadelphian was winning the fight, but his strategy was risky and dangerous—a game plan that could undermine his success at any moment. "He looked like a monster," Chavez said later.

Then, in the middle of the 12th round, it happened. Chavez landed a straight right to the jaw, which forced his opponent into the corner—a man whose battle plan had suddenly betrayed him. The Mexican pursued him, slowly and calmly, sizing him up for one big punch, one final punch. It was a straight right that cracked Taylor on the jaw, sending him to the floor for the first time in his career. Taylor struggled to his feet, grabbing the ropes as if they were lifelines, but the referee looked into his eyes and waved the bout to an end 2 seconds before the final bell—2 seconds before what would have been a victory for the courageous Philadelphian, who was ahead on two of the three scorecards. Taylor lasted 35 minutes and 58 seconds, but it was not enough. "I asked Taylor if he was okay, and I heard no response," referee Richard Steele said afterward. "I wasn't aware of how close we were to the end of the fight. I thought it was more important to figure out if

OPPOSITE: Emblematic of the respect that the two fighters had for each other, this photograph shows Meldrick Taylor (left) and Julio Cesar Chavez trading blows at the outside limit of their reaches during their dramatic contest on March 17, 1990. The fight was decided by the ref with 2 seconds to go in the final round; if time had wound down without interruption, Taylor would have taken the win by decision, though he had clearly suffered more damage.

the kid could go on. I saw a beaten fighter, a young man who had fought his heart out. He got up, but I was not going to let him take another punch."

After the fight, Taylor was admitted to a hospital in Las Vegas, where he was treated for dehydration, a lacerated tongue, and a small fracture in the bone behind his left eye. "Two seconds," he kept repeating in his hospital room. "Two seconds."

## James Toney vs. Michael McCallum
## December 13, 1991

For 36 brutal minutes, James Toney and Michael McCallum created an incredibly intense drama in that theater known as the ring. Then, with one brief announcement, the play collapsed with the most unsatisfying of resolutions—a draw. Toney and McCallum fought to a standstill, with Toney retaining his world middleweight title, but while the decision may have been unsatisfactory, the fight was a brilliant display of boxing at its best.

Toney battered his opponent in the 4th round by landing a three-punch combination—overhand right, left hook, overhand right—that sent McCallum into a clumsy rumba. Then McCallum grabbed the champion and tried to spin him around as if he were a dance partner, a tactic that helped McCallum recover. The challenger landed a crunching left hook that seemed to confuse the champion, who looked down and saw his mouthpiece jutting out of his mouth; Toney inhaled and drew it back inside.

The two men pounded each other in the final rounds. The boxers displayed reservoirs of strength, endurance, and will that astounded the crowd at Convention Hall in Atlantic City. Every punch, every flurry, brought "oohs" and "aahs." Toney almost knocked out the challenger in the final round with a left hook to the jaw that was followed by a volley so furious that he finally stepped back in exhaustion. McCallum would not go down. "I had him hurt in the last 2 rounds, but I just couldn't put him away," Toney said.

OPPOSITE: James Toney (left) and Michael McCallum staged a battle for the ages when they met on December 13, 1991. ABOVE: Michael Moorer (bottom) and Bert Cooper (top) unleashed a cascade of violence against each other in their May 16, 1992, match-up at Trump Plaza in Atlantic City. In the 5th round, Cooper was unsteadily wobbling in an eddy of his own blood when the ref ended the fight, awarding the win to Moorer.

## Michael Moorer vs. Bert Cooper
## May 16, 1992

When Michael Moorer and Bert Cooper make fists, the ringside officials should man an air-raid siren. And when they make fists against each other? Well, they did just that in Atlantic City, and they dropped enough bombs to topple the building in which they were fighting. They fought for something called the World Boxing Organization heavyweight title, but the match was more spectacular than the cheap trinket they were vying for. It was a classic.

It lasted only 15 minutes, but it was 15 minutes of mayhem and brutality. The 1st round compressed 10 rounds of violence into 1, with both fighters landing the kind of punches that would leave most men in body casts. Cooper dropped Moorer early in the round, but when Moorer beat the 10-count, his legs twitching as if from an electrical shock, he rushed at the man who had just pounded him. Moorer landed a two-punch combination to the jaw—chopping left, right hook—and Cooper went down, his head whipping backward like that of a crash-test dummy. It was an incredible display of punching power—2 knockdowns in 3 minutes. But it was not over, not yet.

Cooper dropped his opponent again in the 3rd round, but he returned to his corner with a deep gash over his left eye—the result of an accidental head butt. The two fighters seemed arm-weary in the 4th round, but the shelling was still fearsome, their artillery going from bombs to grenades. In the 5th round, Moorer unloaded about ten straight punches, his final blow a right uppercut that seemed to launch his opponent

halfway across the ring. Cooper landed on his black silk trunks, a part of his wardrobe that had become well acquainted with the canvas. When he barely beat the 10-count, his face shooting a geyser of blood, the referee took one look at his eyes and called a halt to a magnificent bout. The end came 2 minutes and 21 seconds into the round.

### Riddick Bowe vs. Evander Holyfield
### November 13, 1992

They called him "Commander Skylab," a guy who could reach the ozone on the wings of his brash personality. But Riddick Bowe dismissed the criticism—if his head were in the clouds, he said, it was only because his dreams had transported him there. Bowe was right—oh my, was he right—but he had to prove it. Enter Evander Holyfield, the heavyweight champion of the world.

The fighters met in one of the worst eras for heavyweights in history, an era in which the division was filled with fat bellies and fatter paychecks. Ah, but these two fighters took us back to the days of Joe Louis, Rocky Marciano, and Muhammad Ali. Bowe and Holyfield were not legends—not yet, anyway—but they gave boxing fans 36 minutes that would last forever.

Three inches (8cm) shorter and 30 pounds (14kg) lighter than his opponent, Holyfield fought like the bigger man; his spirit overcame his judgment, just as it always did, in fight after fight. He never learned. The champion fought on the inside against the challenger, and he tried—and often succeeded—to jab his way through a minefield of hooks and uppercuts.

In the later rounds, the match became the test of will that most experts had predicted. It was beautiful and ugly, noble and savage, riveting and hard to watch, with both men punching—and taking punches—until most fighters would have collapsed.

Bowe landed a right uppercut to the jaw in the 10th round, a blow that forced the champion into the ropes, where the challenger followed up with about fifteen unanswered punches—hook after hook after hook.

OPPOSITE: Evander Holyfield fends off a crushing right from Riddick Bowe during their legendary first match-up, on November 13, 1992. Though he fought with great courage, Holyfield could not prevail over the larger, stronger Bowe.

The champion refused to go down, his heart keeping him upright just when it seemed his legs would fail him. Then he rallied late in the round by delivering the same brutal punches that he had been absorbing just a few seconds before. It was an incredible exhibition—one of the greatest rounds in heavyweight history. "Suck it up, baby," trainer Lou Duva told the champion between rounds. "And punch like hell."

Bowe dropped the champion with an overhand right in the 11th round, a punch so solid that his opponent crumpled to the canvas, his face frozen in what appeared to be a silent scream. Holyfield scrambled to his feet and grabbed the ropes as the challenger waited in a neutral corner, eager to pound him again. The champion beat the 10-count. "Let's go, Bowe," the crowd roared.

Bowe captured a unanimous decision, jumping wildly when the decision was announced. "Any more questions about his heart?" Rock Newman, who managed Bowe, asked.

Bowe and Holyfield would fight two more times, including the fight with the strangest dive in boxing history—when "Fan Man," a sky diver with a sense of the dramatic, descended from the desert sky into the ring on November 6, 1993, in Las Vegas. Holyfield captured a decision that night, only to get stopped in the 8th round two years later. The fights comprise one of the great trilogies in heavyweight history—right below the Ali-Frazier wars of the 1970s—but it is the first fight that will go down as a classic. "Regardless of how much pressure I put on him, no matter how tired he got, he came back," Holyfield said.

### Arturo Gatti vs. Wilson Rodriguez
### March 22, 1996

They fought for almost 18 brutal minutes. They turned the ring into a back alley with ropes. And when it was all over, the cheers continued long after the punches had stopped. "I'm just happy I won," Gatti, then the junior lightweight champion, said afterward. Happy? He should have been ecstatic. The fighting was so intense that it looked like a battle of attrition from the start—and it was. Both men started out aggressively, punching with a fury that would have exhausted most fighters. Gatti was careless in the 2nd round, and

it was just the opening that Rodriguez wanted—and had anticipated. The champion was a gutsy fighter, and he threw punches without worrying about what he might absorb in return; it made for thrilling—and, for him, dangerous—fighting, because his idea of defense was to smash you with his face before you could smash him with your fists. Exciting? Yes, but the style had cost him his only defeat up to that point—a 6-round loss to King Solomon, a club fighter, four years earlier at the Blue Horizon in Philadelphia.

Gatti displayed the same tendency in fight after fight, recklessly charging at his opponents, his heart and power overcoming his foolishness. But could he withstand the pressure of an opponent who seemed just as tough and strong? Rodriguez seemed to answer that question in the 2nd round, when he dropped the champion onto his yellow silk trunks. The crowd, practically asleep during a miserable undercard at Madison Square Garden, suddenly came to life, cheering wildly as the two warriors threw combination after combination. "When I went down in the 2nd round, I said, 'Oh, my God, I can't believe it,'" Gatti said later.

And the knockdown was just the start of his problems. Gatti absorbed a horrible pounding, his eyes bruised by the end of the 3rd round, his face turning the same shade of red as his gloves. Peering through the slits that his eyes had become, he seemed disoriented, like a man trying to make his way through a dark corridor. But the champion kept punching…and punching…and punching. Then Rodriguez became cocky, wading inside when he could have won the fight by jabbing. Finally, it happened. Gatti landed a left hook to the ribs in the 5th round, a blow that resounded like a drum shot in an empty music studio, and Rodriguez went down, grabbing his side as he fell. The challenger beat the 10-count, but the champion pursued him relentlessly and landed a series of punishing hooks to the body. Gatti finished him in the 6th round with a left hook to the jaw, beating a man who looked like an almost certain winner from the start. "This town will go nuts over Gatti," said Ed Schuyler, Jr., of the Associated Press. "The fans here love fighters with big hearts—like Rocky Marciano."

OPPOSITE: A battered Gatti, who has shown a remarkable ability to weather abuse and still win fights, sits in his corner between rounds.

# The Fight of the Millennium?

They called it "The Fight of the Millennium," a match promised to linger in our memories much longer than the 12 rounds the boxers were scheduled to fight.

In the end, it would be memorable, but more for the disappointment it generated than for the excitement. Blame the hype. Boxing fans crave great fights, great theater, and when they do not get it, they feel bitterness and regret, as if the boxers themselves had let the public down.

It is not the first fight that failed to live up to the hype and it will not be the last. But the Oscar De La Hoya–Felix Trinidad match was supposed to be different. After all, it pitted against each other the two greatest fighters of their era, both undefeated welterweight champions.

Fans expected a brawl, but they saw a tactical match from the beginning, the tension arising not from what was happening as much as from what could happen next. De La Hoya moved from side to side, building up an early lead with a brilliant display of boxing skill. This was not the violent spectacle the fans anticipated; this was a high-priced sparring session. Yes, De La Hoya was boxing beautifully, but his strategy sucked all the drama and excitement out of a match that featured two of the hardest punchers in boxing.

Then De La Hoya, apparently thinking that his lead was comfortable, began to relax in the 10th round, keeping his distance in an effort to preserve what he thought was an easy victory. He should have consulted the judges. As De La Hoya backed up, Trinidad kept moving forward, throwing more punches than he had in the early rounds. It looked like a desperate measure, but would it work?

Despite the shift in momentum during the later rounds, De La Hoya looked like the winner. He boxed well, and he punched sharply and crisply, leaving Trinidad with a bloody nose and a swollen left eye. Nearly 80 percent of the ringside journalists scored the fight for De La Hoya, according to an informal poll by the *Las Vegas Review Journal*.

But if boxing promises anything, it is the unexpected, and this evening was no different. One judge ruled the bout a draw, while the other two scored it for Trinidad—115–113 and 115–114. Trinidad won a majority decision. "I knew he was a great fighter, but I had the will to win," Trinidad said afterward.

De La Hoya was gracious in defeat. "I know I won," he said. "I gave the boxing lesson of my life. People expected me to duke it out, but I was making him miss and making him pay…. I guess it didn't work out."

De La Hoya said he wanted a rematch, and Trinidad said, hmmmm, maybe. "He's a great fighter, and he deserves a rematch, but we'll need to discuss it," Trinidad said.

The fans deserve a rematch, too, but the most brutal battles are often at the negotiating tables, sometimes taking years and years of rancorous wheeling and dealing.

LEFT: Felix Trinidad meets Oscar De La Hoya in their widely anticipated but ultimately disappointing welterweight title bout on September 18, 1999. OPPOSITE: Trinidad celebrates his controversial victory by decision over De La Hoya to win the welterweight crown.

# THE FUTURE OF BOXING

**5**

As a child, I had no doubt that Joe Louis was a greater man than Franklin D. Roosevelt, and in the tales I heard of great heroes, Corbett, Jeffries, Gans, Ketchel, and Dempsey ranked right along with Perseus and Daniel Boone.

—Leonard Gardner, *Fat City*

It is a dangerous game, but every expert plays it, from the television commentators to the couch potatoes who chug their beer as if it were bottled water. They confer greatness upon fighters before fighters are ready to demonstrate that greatness; one terrific fight, one terrific performance, and they start digging the comparisons out of the footlockers that are their brains. He is the next Sugar Ray Robinson, the next Sugar Ray Leonard, the next Muhammad Ali, the next....

Pity the poor pug who has to wear that label—greatness. Why? Because boxing is not like other sports. It is cruel and unforgiving. Roger Clemens may have a bad game or even a bad year, but if he comes back, the experts will shrug their shoulders and say, "See, I told you he was great." But if a boxer has a bad fight or a bad year, he is probably doomed—exiled to a lifetime of undercards in Altoona, Pennsylvania.

Look at Ken Buchanan, the classy Scotsman. He was the lightweight champion of the world, the next Sugar Ray Robinson, until he met a wild man from Panama on June 26, 1972, in New York. Roberto Duran stopped him in the 13th round, pounding him from here to Edinburgh. He hit the champion below the belt in the final round, smashing him so viciously that the protective cup looked like a crumpled fender. Buchanan fell to his knees, unable to continue.

No, when the experts call you "great," it is no cause for celebration. It is a curse. Oh, most fighters do not realize the danger. They love to hear that word, love to hear the comparisons between themselves and the great boxers of the past. But they are wrong—dead wrong. When they hear that word, they should duck. It is worse than any left hook to the temple.

## Floyd Mayweather

If Floyd Mayweather wants to avoid the pitfalls of huge expectations, he just has to look in his corner, where his father, Floyd, Sr., is guiding his career. Is there a better man to lead his son along the right road? Probably not, because a man who has made the wrong decisions for himself knows how to make the right decisions

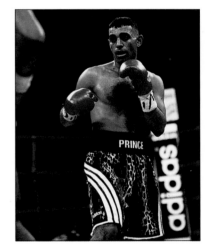

ABOVE: Prince Naseem Hamed of Sheffield, England, boasts extraordinary speed and catlike reflexes—even for a featherweight. If he overcomes his penchant for braggadocio and puts in some serious time with his trainers, he could easily become one of the most spectacular boxers in his generation. OPPOSITE: Floyd Mayweather celebrates his victory over Angel Manfredi on December 13, 1998, in a title bout at the Miccosukee Indian Reservation in Miami, Florida. Mayweather has the potential to become one of the greats of his weight class.

ABOVE: Floyd Mayweather whips a left jab at the head of Carlos Gerena during their September 11, 1999, bout at the Mandalay Bay Resort in Las Vegas, Nevada. Mayweather won the fight by TKO in the 7th round. RIGHT: Angel Manfredi (left) ducks and takes cover during his December 13, 1998, bout against Floyd Mayweather.

for his son. Floyd Sr. served a five-year sentence for drug trafficking, and when his son visited him at the penitentiary in Midland, Michigan, the kid had to fight back his tears. "I was supposed to be a man," the youngster thought. And so he stifled his emotions.

The elder Mayweather, released from prison in 1999, trains his son, and he has done a great job with a great fighter. There is that word again—"great." But father and son are handling it well, refusing to let the praise distract them from their goal, which is, ironically, to achieve greatness. "You never have to make the mistakes I made," the father has told the son. "I made enough for the both of us."

Young but levelheaded, Mayweather comes from a fighting family. His father was a contender, good enough to face Sugar Ray Leonard in 1978, and two of his uncles were talented fighters—one of them, Roger, a two-time world champion. "I taught him to box, and nobody knows or loves him better than me, so nobody's better equipped to take care of him," the elder Mayweather said.

A bronze medalist in the 1996 Olympics in Atlanta, Floyd Mayweather the younger is that rarest of fighters—a flashy boxer with sound technical skills. And power. He is 18-0 as a professional, including an 8th-round knockout of Genaro Hernandez for the world junior lightweight title on October 3, 1998, in Las Vegas. "I'd give myself an eight," Mayweather said of his performance against Hernandez. Hernandez protested. "No one has ever beat me like that,"

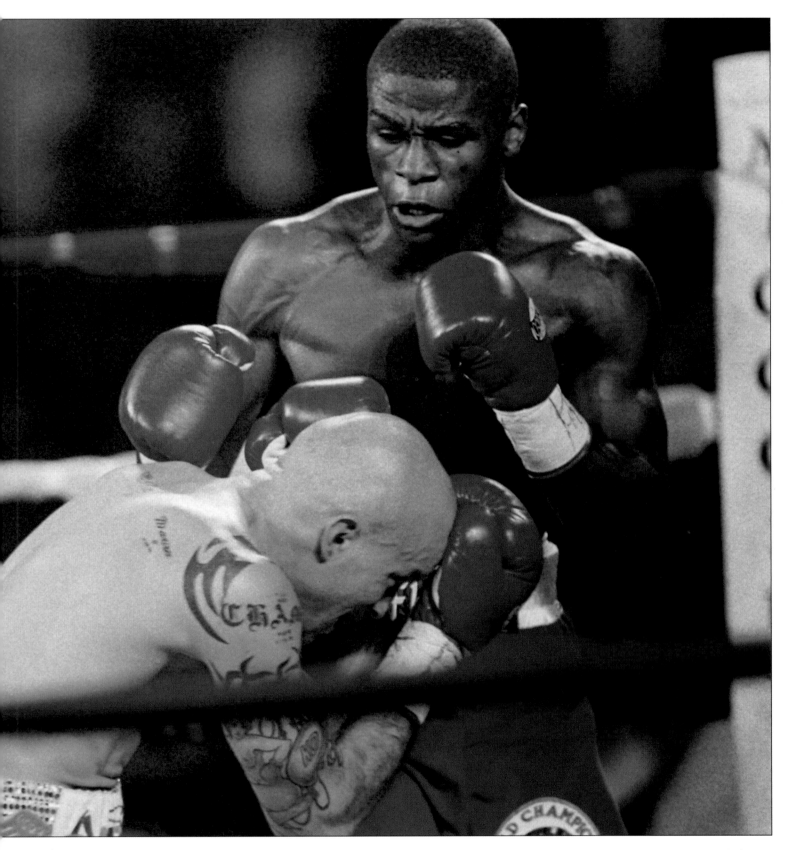

Hernandez said. "So don't you go saying you were an eight, because you were a ten."

A versatile boxer, Mayweather flashed his amazing hand speed throughout the bout, but he also proved that his fists belong in a munitions dump. He pounded his opponent at will by scoring effectively to the body and head. When it was all over, the judges and the referee seemed superfluous, because Hernandez refused to come out for the 9th round, officially ending a fight

that was unofficially over from the start. "I got defeated in a real bad way," Hernandez said. "I never thought I would lose a fight like that. No one has ever hit me the way Floyd Mayweather hit me."

As for Mayweather, he did not let the great performance cloud his vision of the future. "Genaro was a great champion," Mayweather said. "He's the best fighter I've fought to this point. I thank him for the opportunity to fight for the championship."

## Prince Naseem Hamed

A fighter for the MTV generation, Prince Naseem Hamed is a violent man who makes statements with his fists and his outfits, some of which are louder than his personality. He wears leopard-skin trunks, and he leaps over the ropes to enter the ring amid a burst of smoke, lasers, and fireworks—the kind of spectacle common at rock concerts or wrestling matches. But the entrances are not the most outrageous thing about him. No, Hamed is a gaudy talent as well as a gaudy dresser, and he is not above telling you so.

The featherweight champion is 25-0, and if you have a short attention span, he is the fighter for you—of his 23 knockouts, more than half have come before the end of the 2nd round. He won the title with an 8th-round knockout of Tom Johnson on February 7, 1997, in London, when he floored the champion with a right uppercut that seemed to come from the cheap seats. Johnson had defended the crown eleven times, but he had never faced anyone like the Prince. Who has?

Of all the reigning world champions, Hamed may boast the worst technical skills, but he gets away with it. Sure, he drops his hands, punches off the wrong foot, and sticks out his chin. But he boasts crushing power and tremendous reflexes, his showboating lulling you into the serenity that his fists turn into slumber. Just ask Said Lawal. Hamed knocked out Lawal on March 16, 1996, taking only three punches and 35 seconds to complete the demolition. Punch, punch, punch—goodnight.

Hamed grew up in Sheffield, England, but his parents were from Yemen, where the fighter is treated like royalty. He is not a real prince, but he anointed himself one because he figured all true princes must become kings, and he wants to be the king of boxing. Not the king of the featherweights—the king of boxing, period. "Nobody can stand up to the extraordinary power of my fists," he said after stopping Johnson. "I prefer to flatten my opponent in the 2nd round, but my mother said she wanted a little entertainment."

Talented and cocky, Hamed is the heir to fighters such as Hector "Macho" Camacho and Jorge Paez, guys whose fan base included people who wanted to see them get beaten. Hamed is the same way. Love him or hate him, he is the Fresh Prince of boxing.

ABOVE: In typical fashion, Prince Naseem Hamed prances victoriously around the ring at Madison Square Garden after pounding Kevin Kelley into the mat on December 13, 1997. The knockout came in the 4th round, and Kelley's face tells the brief, brutal story of the fight.

## Erik Morales

When he turned 21 on September 1, 1997, Erik Morales refused to celebrate, sacrificing current pleasures for future ecstasies. And oh my, was it ecstasy. The kid waited five days, marking the hours like an inmate awaiting parole, but it was worth it. Morales gave himself the greatest birthday present of his life—a present wrapped in blood, sweat, and grit. He gave himself a world title by stopping Daniel Zaragoza for the junior lightweight crown on September 6 in El Paso. "It was more difficult than I originally thought," Morales said.

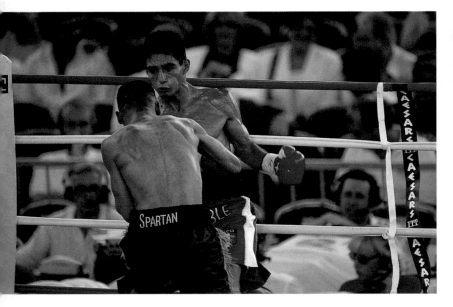

The kid stopped the 40-year-old champion in the 11th round, flooring him with a solid punch to the chest. The old man landed on his butt, sitting on the canvas with his arms wrapped around his knees, in position to perform a sit-up. He sat there for a few seconds, as if contemplating whether to get up and absorb more punishment. Then he shook his head. The old man did not get up; he remained on the canvas, bloody and battered, conceding victory to his young opponent. It was an act of nobility, not cowardice, because the old man fought a tremendous fight, his heart telling him to keep punching long after his body had told him to quit. He finally obeyed his body—his jaw, his ribs, his legs. The crowd of more than six thousand applauded both warriors. "The last punch was a straight right to the solar plexus—and

ABOVE: Erik Morales defends against a stooping, swooping Hector Acero-Sanchez on June 7, 1996, at Caesars Palace. Morales won the fight by decision after 12 tough rounds. The young lightweight promises to become a great fighter in his class. RIGHT: On October 22, 1999, Erik Morales unleashes a sweeping uppercut at the head of Wayne McCullough. The as-yet undefeated Morales won the 12-round unanimous decision over McCullough to successfully defend his WBC super bantamweight crown.

# Christy Martin and the
# Women of Boxing

Christy Martin burst onto the boxing scene on March 16, 1996, in Las Vegas, shocking the boxing world by fighting like, well, a man. But did she fight like a man? Or have men been fighting—from the moment the first two pugilists made fists in a cave—the way Christy Martin would one day fight? It is not a question that Martin herself ponders. Martin is a boxer, not a feminist. She fights for money and respect, not for equal rights. "I'm just happy to be boxing," she said.

Whether or not she wants the label, Martin is a pioneer—as important to boxing as Jackie Robinson was to major league baseball more than forty years ago. If that seems a little far-fetched, it is only because we do not know the full impact of her trailblazing—not yet. But if a woman knocks out some loutish male for the heavyweight title in the year 2025,

we will look back on Martin as a heroic figure.

It may never reach that point, and perhaps it never should. Women fight women, and men fight men, and there is no clamor for intersex matches in the ring. But, then, there was no clamor for female boxing, either. And look at Christy Martin. She is the most famous female boxer in the world, a fighter who is almost universally admired among members of both sexes. When men start talking about female fighters in bars and taverns without snickering, well, you know the women have arrived.

Martin was not an overnight success; it just seems that way. She fought "Dangerous" Deirdre Gogarty on March 16, 1996, in Las Vegas, as part of the undercard for the heavyweight title bout between Mike Tyson and Frank Bruno, which was broadcast throughout the world on pay-per-

OPPOSITE: Christy Martin raises her arms in victory after beating the pulp out of "Dangerous" Deirdre Gogarty on March 16, 1996. Though the fight was an undercard for the heavyweight title bout between Mike Tyson and Frank Bruno, it was much more entertaining to watch. Women's professional boxing may well prove to become a popular facet of the sport, though the final verdict has yet to be handed down. ABOVE: Christy Martin pounds Melinda Robinson into submission during their September 7, 1996, bout in Las Vegas. Martin totally outclassed her opponent and won the fight in the 3rd round by knockout.

view. Martin fought spiritedly—much more spiritedly than Tyson or Bruno—and she became a sensation, wowing fans with her heart and technical skills. She survived a bloody nose to win an easy 6-round decision. "She bled like a stuck pig," said her husband, Jim Martin, who also trains her.

In 1992, Christy Salters walked into a gym in Bristol, Tennessee, accompanied by her mother and her puppy, a Pomeranian. It was the strangest entourage in boxing history but trainer Jim Martin, and a former light heavyweight and self-proclaimed "macho guy," saw something in her that his male fighters lacked—spirit and a desire to learn. And, oh yes, she was tough. The trainer thought, hey, maybe she can make some money for me. After all, she was a novelty, a woman in a world dominated by men. So he helped her learn how to box, later becoming her husband as well as her trainer. "This isn't about women's boxing," Martin said. "This is about Christy Martin."

And she is correct. She has a right to be Christy Martin the individual, not Christy Martin the pioneer. Martin stands 5 feet 4 inches (163cm) and

weighs 133 pounds (60kg), and she is more exciting than most men. She fires short, crisp combinations, every punch thrown with the "bad intentions" that made Tyson such an awesome fighter in the mid-1980s. And she has made money for both herself and her trainer-husband; she earns about $50,000 per bout, as much as Ricardo Lopez, the great strawweight champion, makes. "I would never promote a women's bout," Bob Arum said in 1996. Arum left that to Don King, who promotes Martin. "I'm sorry, but I think women's boxing is repulsive," Arum said.

A few months later, Arum was promoting women on his fight cards, two of whom are beginning to make names for themselves—Lucia Rijker and Mia St. John. And a couple of prodigal daughters have joined the field, too: Laila Ali and Jacqui Frazier. Alas, Jacqui is too old to have much of a career ahead of her, but Ali the younger is in her early twenties and a fighter of great promise.

Martin may not call herself a pioneer, but that's alright: future boxing historians may well do it for her.

it took everything out of him," said Morales, a native of Tijuana. Zaragoza, a native of Mexico City, was gracious afterward: "He simply surprised me with his speed. I did the best I could. I'm not as quick as I used to be."

In a fight full of exhilarating moments, the 8th round was the best. Morales landed two solid rights midway through the round, but the champion remained on his feet and retreated to the ropes, where his young opponent turned him into a heavy bag. The challenger landed a series of punishing blows, but he got tired, his arms so heavy that he could barely raise them. He stepped back to rest, and the champion lifted both gloves and shrugged his shoulders, as if to ask, "Is that all you have?" Then he pursued his opponent across the ring, and the crowd responded with a standing ovation. "I decided to do nothing but body work from the 9th round on," Morales said. After he won the fight, Morales looked back to the days leading up to the big event. "Not only was it my dream to finally win a world title," Morales said, "but the dream is even better since I beat Zaragoza."

And he did it for his birthday.

## David Reid

Every day, the neighborhood kids trooped to the three-story row house in north Philadelphia to gaze at the display in the windows—forty trophies, most of them gold or silver, gleaming like Cadillacs in a showroom. "This is where the fighter lives," the youngsters would say.

That was four years ago, when "the fighter" was the best amateur boxer in Philadelphia, perhaps the best amateur boxer in the world. David Reid is fast becoming one of the best professional boxers in the world, and his window now features another piece of glowing hardware—a championship belt, the World Boxing Association junior middleweight title. "I do what I want to do in the ring," Reid said. "I think clearly, and I don't get tired."

Like Oscar De La Hoya four years earlier, Reid was the only member of the U.S. boxing team to win a gold medal in the 1996 Olympics. It was an amazing performance. Behind 15-5 after 2 rounds, he crushed Alfredo Duvergel with an overhand right to the temple, a blow that knocked the Cuban to his hands and knees in the

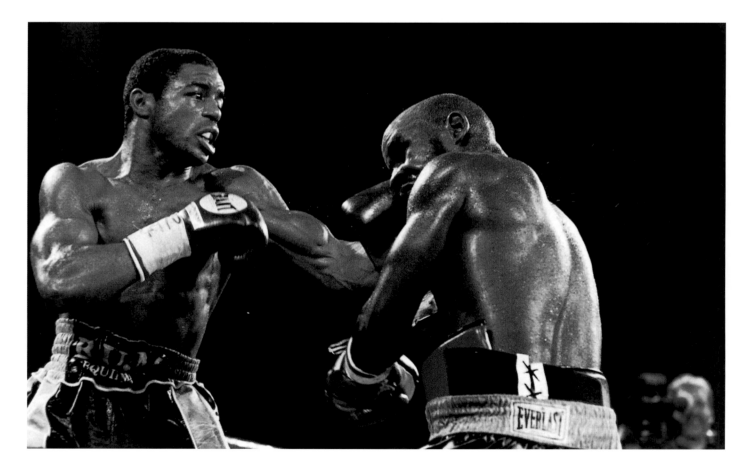

ABOVE: David Reid unleashes a left cross at the head of Keith Mullings at the Hard Rock Hotel, Las Vegas, on his way to the WBA super welterweight championship, August 28, 1999.
OPPOSITE: Junior middleweight David Reid is a smart boxer with awesome physical gifts. And although he is young at this writing, his wisdom—and by extension his promise—is great. Barring the unexpected, Reid should become one of the standout fighters of the era.

3rd round. Duvergel beat the 10-count, but he lurched across the ring and stumbled into the ropes like a drunk at last call. The referee stopped the fight, and Reid jumped into the air—a young man with the vertical leap of an elevator. "I was going for the home run," Reid said. "He hit me hard a couple of times. I said to myself, 'To win, all you need is to get one in.'"

After the gold medal victory, Reid signed a five-year, $30-million contract, including a $1 million signing bonus, with America Presents. "That's only the first of many millions that young man will earn before he is done," said Mat Tinley, owner of the promotional company.

If the money has corrupted him, Reid is hiding it well. The junior middleweight is one of the most ambitious young boxers in the game, and his handlers are equally ambitious, because they matched him with tough opponents instead of soft touches early in his career, including victories over two former world champions—Simon Brown and Jorge Vaca. "As long as they don't let the other guy come in armed, he doesn't care who he fights," said Al Mitchell, his trainer.

It showed. Through his first eleven fights, a critical phase of his career, his opponents boasted a collective record of 272 wins, 43 losses, 4 draws, and 180 knock-outs. Reid is a young man, but his grit and wisdom belie his years. He is becoming a veteran before his time, a smooth boxer with power in both hands. Reid won the World Boxing Association junior middleweight title with a 12-round decision over Laurent Bouduani on March 6, 1999, in Atlantic City. "If this exciting young fighter matures as a professional as expected, and if he wins as we expect him to win, by the year 2001, he could earn $50 million," Tinley said.

ABOVE: Reid receives medical attention for damage to his eye sustained during the March 6, 1999, slugfest against Laurent Boudouani. OPPOSITE: At Bally's Park Place, Atlantic City, Reid hammers Kevin Kelly during their July 16, 1999, match-up.

Reid owes that future to his mother. "He never got into any really bad trouble," said Marie Reid. "But he used to get into fights all the time, and I was afraid he'd get hurt. He was about 10, and I told him to go to the gym. I know most mothers don't like their kids to box, but I wanted him to get off the streets."

Reid did get off the streets, taking his love of mixing it up into a recreation center in north Philadelphia. He enjoyed the indoor fights even more, and there was a good reason: under a policy developed by the boxing coach, Reid could whack his sparring partners, but his sparring partners could not whack him back, which gave the kid the sensation of hitting the heavy bag. That lasted two years. "He loved it," said Fred Jenkins, the coach. "You gotta give young kids a break like that. Boxing is hard enough, and if you make it too hard for the kids, they're gonna sour on it." As good as he is now, if David Reid becomes a great fighter it will be because of what he has yet to overcome. Reid suffered a crushing defeat on March 3, 2000, the first loss of a career that, until then, had looked infinite in its potential. Felix Trinidad dropped the young fighter an astounding four times. "I have to learn from this," Reid said afterward. If he is as good as he seems, he will no doubt profit from the lesson.

# Rankings

Ranking the greatest fighters of all time is a dangerous business, an exercise sure to cause as many fights—or, at least, arguments—as the boxers themselves waged. The following may be such a list. To compile the ratings, we decided to go back in time to an era in which there were only eight weight classes. There are no cruiserweight divisions in these rankings, no junior this and junior that weight categories.

In addition, some fighters were rated in divisions with which they are not normally associated. Gene Tunney, for example, was a tremendous light heavyweight, so we placed him in that category, even though he gained his fame as the world heavyweight champion, the two-time winner over Jack Dempsey. And another heavyweight champ, Ezzard Charles, also excelled as a middleweight and light heavyweight. We rated him in the middleweight category, even though he fought longer in the other divisions.

Finally, because some boxers fought in the junior this and junior that category, you might see them in divisions that seem unfamiliar. We have only one response: we had to put them somewhere.

Again, ranking fighters is a dangerous business. Yet it is somehow irresistible.

## HEAVYWEIGHTS

1. Muhammad Ali (1960–1981) 56–5 with 37 knockouts.
2. Joe Louis (1934–1951) 68–3 with 54 knockouts.
3. Larry Holmes (1973–1997) 65–6 with 42 knockouts.
4. Jack Dempsey (1914–1927) 61–6–8 with 50 knockouts.
5. George Foreman (1969–1998) 76–4 with 68 knockouts.
6. Jack Johnson (1897–1938) 78–13–11 with 49 knockouts.
7. Rocky Marciano (1947–1955) 49–0 with 43 knockouts.
8. Evander Holyfield (1984– ) 35–5 with 25 knockouts.
9. Joe Frazier (1965–1981) 32–4–1 with 27 knockouts.
10. Jersey Joe Walcott (1930–1953) 53–18–1 with 33 knockouts.

## LIGHT HEAVYWEIGHTS

1. Archie Moore (1936–1963) 194–26–8 with 141 knockouts.
2. Michael Spinks (1977–1988) 31–1 with 21 knockouts.
3. Bob Foster (1961–1978) 56–8–1 with 46 knockouts.
4. Tommy Loughran (1919–1937) 96–24–9 with 18 knockouts.
5. Gene Tunney (1915–1928) 65–1–1 with 47 knockouts.
6. Jack O'Brien (1896–1912) 100–7–16 with 46 knockouts.
7. Jack Dillon (1911–1923) 93–6–14 with 61 knockouts.
8. John Henry Lewis (1928–1939) 103–8–6 with 60 knockouts.
9. Maxie Rosenbloom (1923–1939) 208–37–22 with 19 knockouts.
10. Roy Jones (1989– ) 42–1 with 34 knockouts.

## MIDDLEWEIGHTS

1. Sugar Ray Robinson (1940–1965) 175–19–6 with 110 knockouts.
2. Carlos Monzón (1963–1977) 89–3–8 with 61 knockouts.
3. Charley Burley (1937–1950) 74–11–2 with 43 knockouts.
4. Ezzard Charles (1940–1959) 96–25–1 with 58 knockouts.
5. Harry Greb (1913–1926) 115–8–3 with 51 knockouts.
6. Marvelous Marvin Hagler (1973–1987) 62–3–2 with 52 knockouts.
7. Stanley Ketchel (1904–1910) 53–4–5 with 50 knockouts.
8. Emile Griffith (1958–1977) 85–24–2 with 23 knockouts.
9. Jake LaMotta (1941–1954) 83–19–4 with 30 knockouts.
10. Mickey Walker (1919–1939) 93–19–4 with 60 knockouts.

## WELTERWEIGHTS

1. Henry Armstrong (1931–1945) 151–21–9 with 101 knockouts.
2. Sugar Ray Leonard (1977–1997) 36–3–1 with 25 knockouts.
3. Barney Ross (1929–1938) 74–4–3 with 24 knockouts.
4. Julio Cesar Chavez (1980– ) 101–3–2 with 85 knockouts.
5. Jimmy McLarnin (1923–1936) 63–11–3 with 20 knockouts.
6. Jose Napoles (1956–1975) 77–7 with 54 knockouts.
7. Aaron Pryor (1976–1990) 39–1 with 35 knockouts.
8. Fritzie Zivic (1931–1949) 157–65–10 with 81 knockouts.
9. Kid Gavilan (1943–1958) 107–30–6 with 28 knockouts.
10. Ted "Kid" Lewis (1909–1929) 169–30–13 with 70 knockouts.

## LIGHTWEIGHT

1. Roberto Duran (1967–1999) 102–15 with 69 knockouts.
2. Tony Canzoneri (1925–1939) 138–23–10 with 44 knockouts.
3. Benny Leonard  (1911–1932) 89–5–1 with 71 knockouts.
4. Joe Gans (1891–1909) 120–8–10 with 55 knockouts.
5. Ike Williams (1940–1955) 123–25–5 with 60 knockouts.
6. Alexis Arguello (1974–1995) 80–8 with 64 knockouts.
7. Kid Chocolate (1928–1938) 135–9–6 with 51 knockouts.
8. Pernell Whitaker (1984– ) 40–3–1 with 17 knockouts.
9. Beau Jack (1940–1955) 83–24–5 with 40 knockouts.
10. Battling Nelson (1896–1917) 60–19–19 with 32 knockouts.

## FEATHERWEIGHTS

1. Willie Pep (1940–1966) 230–11–1 with 65 knockouts.
2. Salvador Sanchez (1975–1982) 44–1–1 with 32 knockouts.
3. Sandy Saddler (1944–1956) 144–16–2 with 103 knockouts.
4. Terry McGovern (1887–1908) 59–4–4 with 34 knockouts.
5. Abe Attell (1900–1917) 92–10–16 with 48 knockouts.
6. Wilfredo Gomez (1974–1989) 42–3–1 with 40 knockouts.
7. Azumah Nelson (1985–1996) 39–3–2 with 28 knockouts.
8. Eusebio Pedroza (1973–1992) 42–6–1 with 25 knockouts.
9. Danny Lopez (1971–1992) 42–6 with 39 knockouts.
10. Sergio Palma (1976–1990) 52–5–5 with 21 knockouts.

## BANTAMWEIGHTS

1. Ruben Olivares (1965–1988) 88–13–3 with 78 knockouts.
2. Eder Jofre (1957–1976) 72–2–4 with 50 knockouts.
3. Carlos Zarate (1970–1988) 61–4 with 58 knockouts.
4. Manuel Ortiz (1938–1955) 96–28–3 with 49 knockouts.
5. Panama Al Brown (1922–1942) 124–19–10 with 55 knockouts.
6. Khaosai Galaxy (1980–1991) 49–1 with 43 knockouts.
7. Fighting Harada (1960–1970) 55–7 with 22 knockouts.
8. Orlando Canizales (1984– ) 50–5–1 with 37 knockouts
9. Lupe Pintor (1974–1995) 56–14–2 with 42 knockouts.
10. Jeff Chandler (1976–1984) 33–2–2 with 18 knockouts.

## FLYWEIGHTS

1. Jimmy Wilde (1911–1923) 126–4–2 with 77 knockouts.
2. Miguel Canto (1969–1982) 61–9–4 with 15 knockouts.
3. Frankie Genaro (1920–1934) 82–21–8 with 19 knockouts.
4. Pascual Perez (1952–1964) 84–7–1 with 57 knockouts.
5. Benny Lynch (1931–1938) 82–13–15 with 33 knockouts.
6. Humberto "Chiquita" Gonzalez (1984–1995) 41–3 with 29 knockouts.
7. Hilario Zapata (1977–1993) 43–10–1 with 15 knockouts.
8. Jung-Koo Chang (1980–1991) 38–4 with 17 knockouts.
9. Michael Carbajal (1990–1998) 44–4 with 29 knockouts.
10. Yoko Gushiken (1974–1981) 23–1 with 15 knockouts.

# Selected Bibliography

Anderson, Dave. *In the Corner: Great Boxing Trainers Talk About their Art*. New York: William Morrow & Company, Inc., 1991.

Cannon, James J. *Nobody Asked Me, but... The World of Jimmy Cannon*. New York: Holt Rinehart Winston, 1978.

Greenberg. Martin H., ed. *In the Ring: A Treasury of Boxing Stories*. New York: Bonanza Books, 1986.

Heinz, W.C. *Once They Heard the Cheers*. New York: Doubleday, 1979.

Hughes, Bill, and Patrick King, eds. *Come Out Writing: A Boxing Anthology*. London: Macdonald Queen Anne Press, 1991.

Isenberg, Michael T. *John L. Sullivan and His America*. Chicago and Urbana, IL: University of Illinois Press, 1988.

Leibling, A.J. *A Neutral Corner: Boxing Essays*. San Francisco: North Point Press, 1990.

—————. *The Sweet Science*. New York: Viking Press, 1956.

McIlvanney, Hugh. *McIlvanney on Boxing*. New York: Beaufort Books, Inc., 1982.

Mead, Chris. *Champion Joe Louis: Black Hero in White America*. New York: Scribner's, 1985.

Miletich, Leo N. *Dan Stuart's Fistic Carnival*. College Station, TX: Texas A&M University Press, 1994.

Oates, Joyce Carol, and Daniel Halpern, eds. *Reading the Fights*. New York: Henry Holt, 1988.

Schulian, John. *Writers' Fighters and Other Sweet Scientists*. Kansas City: Andrews and McMeel, 1983.

Smith, Red. *Press Box: Red Smith's Favorite Sports Stories*. New York: W.W. Norton & Company, 1976.

Sporting News. *Best Sports Stories, 1989 Edition*. St. Louis: The Sporting News Book Publishing, 1989.

Sugar, Bert Randolph. *The 100 Greatest Boxers of All Time*, revised updated edition. New York: Bonanza Books, 1989.

Walsh, Peter. *Men of Steel: The Lives and Times of Boxing's Middleweight Champions*. London: Robson Books, 1993.

Weston, Stanley, and Steven Farhood. *The Ring: Boxing, the 20th Century*. New York: BDD Illustrated Books, 1993.

Weston, Stanley, ed. *The Best of the Ring: Recapturing 70 Years of Boxing Classics*. Chicago: Bonus Books, Inc. 1992.

# Index

## A

Acero-Sanchez, Hector, *144*
African Americans, and boxing, *26*, 30, 35–36,
         111–112
Ali, Layla, 148
Ali, Muhammad, 10–11, 50–57, *50–53, 55*
         and Angelo Dundee, 104–106, *104*
         boxing style, 9, 17, 29
         and Larry Holmes, 78–80
         and "Rumble in the Jungle," 9, *12, 53,* 74–78, 111
         *vs.* Foreman, 9, *12, 53,* 74–78, 111
         *vs.* Frazier, 120–122, *121*
         *vs.* Marciano, 46–47
         *vs.* Moore, 48
Ambers, Lou, 43, *43,* 44
Andries, Dennis, 109
Antuofermo, Vito, 70, *71*
Arcel, Ray, 106
Arguello, Alexis, 103, 124–126, *125*
Armstrong, Harry, 42
Armstrong, Henry "Hammerin' Hank," 42–44, *43*
Art, boxing as, 17
Arum, Bob, 78, 82, 102, 112–113, *112,* 148
Atkins, Claudell, 84
Atlas, Teddy, 59, 86, *114*
Avna, Marcela, *101*

## B

Bare-knuckle boxing, 18, 23, *24–25,* 26
Basilio, Carmen, *39,* 106
Benitez, Wilfred, *62*
Benton, George, *9,* 42, 52–57, 89, 107–108, *107*
Berbick, Trevor, 84
Berger, Meyer, 35
Biggs, Tyrell, 84, 114
Bimstein, Whitey, 106
Black, Julius, *36*
Bouduani, Laurent, 152
Bowe, Riddick, 95, *95, 102,* 103, 132–134, *133*
Boxing
         ancient forms of, 17–18, *18*
         as art, 17
         beauty of, 9
         brutality of, 9–13, 117
         excitement of, 117
         history of, 17–27
         legality of, 27
         social standing of, 15–16, 17
         styles of, and body styles, 29–30
Braddock, James J., *36,* 37
Bramble, Livingstone, 114
Braxton, Dwight, 94
Breland, Mark, 114
Broughton, Jack, 19

Brown, Drew, *104*
Brown, Simon, 152
Buchanan, Ken, *56,* 59, 139
Bumphus, Johnny, 114
Burns, Tommy, *26,* 30

## C

Camacho, Hector "Macho," 62, 65–66, 142
Cannon, Jimmy, 15, 17, 37
Carpentier, Georges, 27, *27,* 110
Carter, Rubin "Hurricane," *9*
Championships, proliferation of, 21
Champs Gym, 101
Chance, Dean, 21
Charles, Ezzard, 37–39, 46
Charpentier, Patrick, 113
Chavez, Julio Cesar, 9, *28,* 88–90, *88–90,* 91, 111
         boxing style, 30
         trainers for, 109
         *vs.* Meldrick, 128–131, *129*
Chuvalo, George, 29
Clancy, Gil, 86
Cobb, Irvin S., 110
Cobb, Randall "Tex," 21
Coffrath, Jim, *31*
Collins, Nigel, 113
Conn, Billy, *vs.* Louis, 119–120, *119*
Cooney, Gerry, *75,* 77, 80, 103
Cooper, Bert, *vs.* Moorer, 131–132, *132*
Corbett, "Gentleman" Jim, *23,* 27
Cut men, 113

## D

D'Amato, Cus, 86
De la Hoya, Oscar, *2,* 90, 91–92, *91*
         promotion of, 113
         trainers for, 109
         *vs.* Trinidad, *2, 136,* 137, *137*
Demarco, Tony, 106
Dempsey, Jack, 32–35, *32, 33, 100, 109*
         *vs.* Carpentier, 27, *27,* 110
         *vs.* Willard, 32, 37, *116,* 118–119, *118*
Deshong, Andrea, *148*
Douglas, Billy, 87, 88
Douglas, James "Buster," 84, *85,* 86–88, *87,* 92, *94,*
         107, 112
Douglas, John Sholto, *16,* 19
Doyle, Arthur Conan, 29
Dundee, Angelo, *50,* 59, 70, 103, 104–106, *104, 105*
Duran, Roberto, *56–60,* 57–62, *117,* 139
Durelle, Yvon, 48
Duva, Dan, 77, 113–114, *114*
Duva, Kathy, 114
Duva, Lou, 91, *107,* 113–114, *114,* 134
Duvergel, Alfredo, 150–152

## Photo Credits